Parent-Child Retreats

Spiritual Experiences
for Children Ages 7-10 and Their Parents

Lynne Knickerbocker

Maggie Pike

Mary Ann Figlino, CSJ

Eleanor Sheehan, CSJ

Foreword by
Barbara Campbell

We dedicate this book to the children in our lives,
who have shown us the love of Jesus in its purest form:

Karen, Sara, and Adam Knickerbocker
Tim, Anne, Betsy, Andrew, and Molly Pike
Lisa and Angie Figlino
Emily, Claire, and Elizabeth Sheehan

Our love and deepest gratitude to Steve Pike, Bob Knickerbocker, Janet Figlino,
and Wendy Ebert for their support, encouragement, and creative contributions.

Special thanks to our editor, Kathy Coffey, who wouldn't let up,
but always persisted with kindness and humor.

©1998 by Lynne Knickerbocker, Maggie Pike, Mary Ann Figlino, Eleanor Sheehan

The scripture quotations used herein are taken from the Contemporary English Version,
copyright ©1995 American Bible Society, and are used by permission.

Living the Good News, Inc.
a division of The Morehouse Group
Editorial Offices
600 Grant Street, Suite 400
Denver, CO 80203

Cover Design and Layout: Val Price
Illustrations: Blanche Sims
Diagrams: Anne Kosel

Printed in the United States of America.

ISBN 1-889108-37-5

"People were bringing even infants to him

that he might touch them."

Luke 18:15

Foreword

The family is the foundation of the human community. Support for this fundamental reality is becoming ever more important as the pressures on family life constantly increase. Teachers and leaders at all levels in parishes and schools are continually searching for practical, realistic ways to provide that support.

In his Letter on *The Role of the Christian Family in the Modern World*, Pope John Paul II calls husband and wife, parents and children, "...to live with fidelity the reality of communion in a constant effort to develop an authentic community of persons." *(Role #18)* This is no small task in today's world. Speaking to the essential principles for Christian families, the pope notes that the fundamental opportunity for building the reality of this communion of persons is "constituted by the educational exchange between parents and children in which each gives and receives." *(Role #18)* Parents who use their skills as teachers and loving listeners to their children are also those most likely to, in the words of John Paul II, "...maintain a living awareness of the 'gift' they continually *receive from their children*" *(Role #18)* (emphasis added). What a perfect example of that sense of being gifted is found in the authors' dedication of this work to "...the children who have shown us the love of Jesus in its purest form." Christian parents who are aware of their children as 'gift' create an atmosphere of acceptance, love, and esteem. Children who live in an environment such as this "...are able to grow in wisdom and in stature, and in favor with God and man..." offering "...their own precious contribution to building up the family community...." *(Role #26)*

The retreats in this book provide just the help needed to build up the family community and establish the environments that make it possible for children and parents to contribute to each other's growth in faith. Building on the successful strategies developed in *Parent-Child Retreats: Spiritual Experiences for Children Ages 3-6 and Their Parents*, these creative authors have provided further opportunities for families to grow as their children continue to mature. A rich variety of models for how the retreats can be structured makes this an adaptable resource, valuable for use in many settings: Reconciliation and Eucharist retreats, especially important for this age group; retreats for children with their parents; or children's retreats designed for parent follow-up at home.

As in the first book, the retreats in this second volume are built on solid theological and psychological foundations. This is key both for understanding children's openness to the grace of God and for honoring the unique ways each age group develops. In his letter on families, Pope John Paul II emphasizes the role of the Christian family in presenting all those topics necessary for leading children to maturity as Christians. The topics that he highlights include: introducing children into the mystery of salvation and learning to adore God in Spirit and truth. He stresses that children, and all family members, need to learn to grow in order to "conduct their personal life in true righteousness and holiness according to their true nature." *(Role #39)* Even a quick look at the table of contents of *Parent-Child Retreats* shows that these ideals are being addressed with practical and well thought-out experiences and reflections.

As we see here, help is not simply on the way, help has arrived. With *Parent-Child Retreats: Spiritual Experiences for Children Ages 7-10 and their Parents* along with their previous book *Parent-Child Retreats: Spiritual Experiences for Children Ages 3-6 and their Parents*, these insightful authors have gifted families and the Church with strategies filled with hope for creating environments of grace for all who participate in them. In this they are helping to fulfill the hopes of John Paul II for creating the Christian family "…that is open to transcendent values, that serves its brothers and sisters with joy, that fulfills its duties with generous fidelity, and is aware of its daily sharing in the mystery of the glorious Cross of Christ." *(Role #53)*

—Dr. Barbara Campbell,
Director of Catechetical Services, Loyola Press,
formerly Associate Director, Dept. of Religious
Education, NCEA

Contents

Overview

Ten years ago, when our children were toddlers and preschoolers, we managed to get away for the first weekend retreat we'd attended since high school. We'd be less than honest if we tried to present ourselves as holy women seeking spiritual truth at the nearby house of prayer. Actually, the promise of two nights of uninterrupted sleep and six meals prepared by someone else, not to mention those same someone elses washing our dishes, drew us to retreat that weekend. Typical of the Holy Spirit's ways, the weekend was grace-filled and sent us to our homes refreshed, renewed, and so uplifted that we didn't pull our hair out when one of our little ones asked, "Why did you go to the retreat without *me?*"

Our own experience of the transformation that comes from spending time with God got us thinking and talking. Are adults and teenagers the only ones capable of intimacy with Jesus?

The retreat movement was aimed at these age groups, overlooking, we felt, the natural ability of younger children to grasp the Divine. Their intuition, spontaneity, and friendly openness are qualities that make the deepest friendships. Why not encourage a friendship with Jesus? We entertained the possibility that our children actually *could* have been on retreat with us, that in the shared experience we both might have deepened our friendship with our loving God.

So we acted on our hunch. We began giving retreats for three- to six-year-olds and their parents. We found these young retreatants were eager to be there, enthusiastic in their friendship with Jesus, and profound in their understanding of the presence and action of God in their lives. Even today, teenagers tell us what they remember about retreats they made as preschoolers. Because they've been doing this from early on, they perceive retreats as a natural part of life. This had been our hope indeed.

Eventually we wrote a book to share these experiences with a wider audience. *Parent-Child Retreats: Spiritual Experiences for Children Ages 3-6 and Their Parents* (Living the Good News, 1997) sparked the interest of parents and religious educators across the country. Many wondered why it had not been written years ago.

Parents, initially surprised there was such a thing as a retreat *only* for their preschoolers, wanted the same for their older children. At first we noticed parents "sneaking" their over-six-year-olds into the retreats. Then they began asking if their older children could come as helpers. Finally, inevitably, they begged us to plan the retreats so the whole family could participate.

So here it is. We've written *Retreats for Children Ages 7-10* to be used in a variety of ways. When used alone, these nine ready-to-give retreats are a resource for churches and schools as they provide spiritual experiences for children seven- to ten years old *and* their parents, or retreats for children *only*, with parent follow-up at home. When used in conjunction with *Parent-Child Retreats: Spiritual Experiences for Children Ages 3-6 and Their Parents*, a family retreat can take place. Two of the retreats are ideal for sacramental preparation, and include parent preparation talks as well for Eucharist and Reconciliation.

The Foundation

Children have tremendous potential for grasping spiritual truth if it's presented at their developmental level and rooted in their experience. In his book *Open Mind, Open Heart*, Father Thomas Keating presents forty-two "Guidelines for Christian Life, Growth and Transformation," rooted in scripture, his effort to restate the Christian spiritual journey in contemporary terms.[1] The themes of our retreats are founded on these spiritual principles. At the beginning of each retreat, we state three or four aspects of a theme, which correspond to Keating's guidelines.

How to Use The Retreats

These nine retreats are written for seven- to ten-year-olds. The adult team leaders facilitate the retreat experience and the adult-child sharing afterwards. The retreats can be presented during school time, in the evening, or on the weekend. Each one is two hours long. Three adult facilitators are necessary, with two or three extra adult helpers, to insure the smooth flow of the retreat. A maximum of thirty children is ideal. We find it better to give the retreat three times for a group of thirty than to give one retreat for ninety children.

We encourage retreat directors, classroom teachers, and religion teachers to elevate this experience of Jesus in the eyes of the participants. Doctrine will undoubtedly be taught during religion class, but a retreat is an experience of the friendship of Jesus. Therefore, the format and setting of the retreat should differ from that of a religion class. The format we provide should suffice, but adaptations for a school's particular situation are appropriate.

The retreat should avoid any resemblance to an academic activity. A change of location, therefore, might prove beneficial to establishing a festive atmosphere for spending special time with a good friend, Jesus. The gym, auditorium, and cafeteria are possibilities, as are classrooms where the children don't normally gather.

Schools and parishes favor different groupings for the retreats. Some present the retreat to seven- to ten-year-olds in mixed-age groups. Others prefer to keep same-age children together. Again, it's important not to have groups so large that adult-child sharing is hampered. So, too, it is important to instill sensitivity in and to monitor the children in cross-graded retreats so the older children don't dominate.

If a school decides to give retreats by grade, the ratio of adults to children should be no larger than 1:15. If more than one class is involved, the children may be grouped so members of different classes are mixed, or a teacher may like to see her class bond within itself in this special way. Before grouping children, it's advisable to consult among the adult leaders and teachers.

All children gather at the beginning for the introduction to the theme of the retreat. Children are wearing nametags of three different colors or designs, so when it's time to break into groups, they join their nametag group. If the children are different ages, same-aged children might wear the same colored nametags so the children can stay together for the activities. Each adult facilitator takes her group to a predetermined room or area, where she leads them in prayer through art, story, or the heart room prayer. The children rotate activities after each twenty-minute session, staying with the same group. All groups converge for a communal snack following the prayer activities, then regroup with adult leaders for sharing time. (See Chapter 2, "What We Do and Why We Do It" for more detail.)

We recommend a positive, enthusiastic approach to the event, with publicity school-wide and letters of explanation sent to parents encouraging their support. Some schools make posters announcing the retreat and, later, encouraging the retreatants. Others invite older or younger students to write notes to retreatants, offering their prayers. Children catch excitement and grasp the power of the retreat experience when they're surrounded by a contagious enthusiasm.

Some parishes will want to have a family retreat, which would include younger siblings. In this case, the retreats can be coordinated with those in *Parent-Child Retreats: Spiritual Experiences for Children Ages 3-6 and Their Parents* (Living the Good News, 1997). The retreats have similar themes, and the schedules are the same. Again, another choice presents itself. Because the introductory presentations for preschoolers and school-aged children differ in focus, the directors can choose one gathering presentation for the entire family, or present the different focus talks after dividing the children into age groups.

When parents are present at retreats, a fourth leader is needed to give the adult presentation. The Eucharist and Reconciliation retreats, which may be used as retreats for sacramental preparation, include a talk for parents directly related to those retreats. Three additional parent session outlines, which are not specific to any particular retreat, are also included in this book. The seven adult retreats provided in *Parent-Child Retreats: Spiritual Experiences for Children Ages 3-6 and Their Parents* (Living the Good News, 1997) are additional resources. The outlines for parent sessions cover basic spiritual truths to help parents in their call to be the primary religious educators of their children.

When parents do not attend the retreat with their children, we provide follow-up in the form of a letter explaining the retreat experience and inviting parents to share some of the same experiences with their child at home. *(See Appendix.)* This time together at home need not be formal and structured. Parent and child can choose a time when neither is preoccupied, and a location that is inviting and conducive to visiting with one another. A retreat is an experience of Jesus' friendship, which children know first through intimacy in the family. It's a way of life rather than a single activity.

Why Have Parent Involvement in Children's Retreats?

We encourage schools and churches to involve parents in retreats with their children. When our oldest children were preparing for Eucharist at their Catholic school, several parents gathered on the playground to commiserate. "They want *us* to teach them at home," moaned one particularly adamant parent. "I'm not for it. *They* should do it—that's why we send our kids here." Some parents lack confidence in being their children's primary religious educators, perhaps remembering days when they couldn't get their catechism answers just right. We base this book on the premise that doctrine will be taught in school or religious education classes and that religion teachers will provide the parents with doctrinal materials when supplementary teaching is required.

This book, however, emphasizes the spiritual experience of responding to Jesus' invitation to a love relationship. This experience means loving God, each other, and ourselves as a way of life and, in so doing, growing in the fruits of the Holy Spirit. It's a life balanced with doing and being, that is, serving others and being a presence of God's love to the people in our lives. The nourishment for this way of life is periodic retreats.

With parental involvement in children's retreat experiences, we offer an opportunity to initiate parents and children into sharing faith and prayer with each other. We encourage openness and honesty on both parts. Parents need not hesitate to admit difficulty in prayer, for example. What children need to hear is that their parents have a desire for friendship with Jesus and that they're willing to devote time to that relationship. Both children and parents will recognize the importance of a daily routine of "showing up" in prayer.

Family retreats reinforce that we are the church. Our young members are not the future church, but the current church. When parents make retreats with their children, or share the spiritual experience at home, they add importance to the retreat and meaning to the communal aspect of church. When we give family retreats in schools and parishes we're always delighted to watch children during the potluck dinner, connecting with each other as they run around, faces lighted, while their parents visit, not unlike a holiday with the cousins at a favorite relative's. The connectedness of all ages of believers is an experience of God's people.

Therefore, even when parents don't make the retreat with their children, we offer opportunities to share the retreat experience with follow-up activities at home. Some schools or parishes may wish to extend an invitation to parents to an informal reception following the retreat, either on the same day or later in the week. Whenever parents and children gather in God's name, the power is palpable and memories are formed.

Classroom Follow-up

The school or parish, too, may wish to extend the retreat with follow-up over the ensuing days or weeks. Teachers have more than enough curriculum to cover, we realize, but "follow-up" can be as simple as a student-made bulletin board carrying the theme of the retreat or an occasional return to the heart room prayer. Teachers might set aside a few minutes during part of the day for children to share their experiences of the presence and action of God in their lives. They've encountered a loving Jesus in their retreat, and any follow-up should reinforce awareness that Jesus continues to invite them into a love relationship.

For some children the friendship of Jesus will be confusing. Children who are not raised in loving homes, for example, may not understand the concept of unconditional love. Their only knowledge of love is based on the imperfect model they've known from their caretakers. The precepts of the retreat, therefore, may take a long time to unfold and to internalize. Reinforcement at school can help this process.

Forming a Team

In children's retreats, all activities—craft, story, and prayer—are expressions of prayer when facilitated in a prayerful spirit by team leaders. These directors should have some basic qualifications: a love and respect for children, an excitement about their own relationship with a loving Jesus, and an ability to see spiritual meaning in ordinary life. Practically, they must have a sense of responsibility for children and agree to adhere to the time frames. Religion teachers might fill the bill, or to give the retreat an air of uniqueness, schools may choose to recruit the Director of Religious Education, the pastor, or other adults significant to the children's lives: grandparents, parents, the school nurse, the coach, the youth director. Confirmation candidates or young people who have made retreats before make wonderful assistants to the team, and give retreatants the affirmation that they are important.

Profiles of Children Ages Seven to Ten

It's important that all team members be knowledgeable about the nature of children. We keep in mind their developmental level at all times and don't hesitate to make changes, even midstream, if what we're doing isn't suited to it.

Children learn by seeing, hearing, and touching, and they retain more in their long-term memory if they are active participants rather than passive listeners. We attempt to provide a variety of activities that will appeal to visual, auditory, and tactile learners. In planning and delivering our children's retreats, we follow these two rules religiously: Keep it simple and remain flexible.

To assist in planning retreats appropriate to the age level of our retreatants, we include the profiles of seven- to ten-year-olds from the curriculum series *This Is Our Faith*.[2]

Ages 7-8

Children this age:
▲ are active, inquisitive, and full of life
▲ are more sure of themselves after one or two years of regular school
▲ are still dependent on the guidance and approval of their parents, teachers, and other adults
▲ pay attention one moment, then daydream the next

▲ have difficulty thinking back logically to why something happened; may respond to logic with blank stares

▲ have difficulty thinking abstractly

▲ tend to be self-centered; may have difficulty sharing

▲ have short emotional fuses when their desires are not fulfilled

Ages 9-10

Children this age:

▲ are mastering the ability to read and enjoy using this skill

▲ are able to learn more readily from their observations of life, nature, and people

▲ have increased reasoning ability

▲ have an increased social sense and place great emphasis on friendship

▲ are sensitive about being embarrassed or criticized in front of their friends

▲ need to belong to a group, particularly a family group, where they receive love and acceptance

▲ need to work with adults to accomplish a goal, yet sometimes resist with talking back or anger, motivated by their move towards independence

▲ are able to make moral decisions

Tips for Directing Children

Through trial and error, we've discovered some tricks which have helped us engage children in large groups and focus the ones who get distracted. No matter what the child's behavior, we try to discover the need behind it and respond to that need, rather than ignore or scold the child.

▲ Encourage all retreatants to sit close together.

▲ Throughout the retreat, inform the children of what's going to happen before it happens.

▲ Use the children's names frequently. Read them right off their nametags.

▲ Maintain eye contact in both large and small groups.

▲ Occasionally change volume or tone, or move about for variety.

▲ Include the children's comments in the presentation.

▲ Ask the children to repeat a short phrase.

▲ Get the group's attention by saying in a hushed voice, "Listen carefully. I have something important to tell you."

▲ Ask a distracted child to help you in some way.

▲ Walk over to a talkative child, put your hand on his or her shoulder, and continue talking.

▲ Provide a variety of different kinds of activities within the twenty-minute sessions: drawing, singing, or acting out a play.

▲ Review important points to remember.

▲ Involve children with objects and experiences that appeal to the senses: smell, taste, and touch.

▲ Present one idea at a time and surround it with experiences that are relevant to the children.

▲ Involve the children in sharing activities, such as distributing materials, using supplies together, and cleaning up together.

Guidelines for the Parent Sessions

While the focus of our retreats is on seven-to-ten-year-old children, the parents also appreciate their time together, a time to renew their own spirituality. Since our parent session lasts only fifty to sixty minutes, we want to ensure that our adult retreatants gain the most during their brief time together.

In planning our parents' session, therefore, we draw on the advice of adult educator Dolores Curran, who has recorded her experiences and insights from facilitating successful parent groups in her book, *Working with Parents*.[3] The following tips can assist the retreat director in planning the parents' session of a family retreat.

Know the interests and concerns of the group.

Our own presentations have developed from the needs of our participants, but our focus is always on young children and on the parents themselves in their call to be their children's first teachers. Within this context, it's important to invite the retreatants' suggestions for topics, either informally in conversation, or by means of a formal survey. The parents' session is enriched by the input of the participants themselves.

It's the responsibility of the retreat team to listen to the parents' interests. Adults seek our family retreats for companionship with other parents who share the same values, uncertainty about how to share their faith with their young children, concern about their teenager who is rejecting traditional religion, personal spiritual nourishment, and any other number of reasons. All are valid and the retreat team gives value to the needs of parents by addressing their concerns during the adult retreat session.

Create a pleasing environment.

To create a sacred atmosphere we design a focal point, such as a small table with flowers, a picture, the Bible, a candle, or whatever might be aesthetically pleasing to our retreatants. As the eyes rest upon it, the focal point is a reminder of God's gentle presence in the room. A pleasing environment contributes to the building of a community among retreatants. Placing the chairs in a circle or semi-circle invites eye contact and promotes interaction among retreatants. The director facilitates bonding within the group by encouraging parents to sit close together, filling in empty seats.

Since our adult membership is fairly small—twenty-five is typical—we don't normally need a microphone. However, when we do use one for larger groups, we test it ahead of time to make sure we know how it works and whether the volume is adequate for the size of the room.

Be true to your own personality.

In making a presentation, we are most effective when we use our own unique gifts: strong delivery, gentleness, humor, gregariousness, or visible spirituality. Whether a speaker uses notes or not, God works through a person's uniqueness. Trying to be something we are not poses a barrier to the flow of the Spirit.

Know your subject.

Whether from first-hand experience or from extensive talking with parents, as well as from reading, the adult leader must be familiar with family life in order to effectively lead parents in reflection on their own spiritual leadership in the family.

Even if the speakers have not raised children, it is important that they understand and appreciate parenthood. Retreatants expect the director to be knowledgeable about parents' role in the faith development of their children.

Control the agenda.

It's the director's role to keep the topic on focus, prevent participants from monopolizing the discussion, and avert digressions into areas unrelated to the retreat. A comment like, "I sense the group is ready to get back to the topic. Am I right?" or a light-hearted, "Well, time to talk about [the topic] again" can be most effective in regaining control of the agenda.

Empower the retreatants.

People retain more in their long-term memory if they are active participants rather than passive listeners. The retreat director, who is chiefly responsible for the content of the parents' session presentation, empowers the parents to share their insights with each other. Retreatants add wisdom that enriches the retreat many-fold.

If a group seems reluctant to speak, is overly chatty, or if a few people dominate the discussion, the director can try the technique of stopping the presentation periodically and posing a question, inviting participants to share with the person next to them. A discussion with the larger group might follow, or it might be saved until the end of the talk. This opportunity for paired reflection helps retreatants to focus their thoughts before sharing with the whole group, and empowers those who hesitate to speak before large groups to express their thoughts as well.

Use simple language rather than professional jargon.

Using professional language distances the speaker from participants and is counterproductive to the goal of encouraging parents to share their insights and experiences with each other. Theological terms, for example, are not always familiar to people, not universally understood, and often vary among churches. Common experience, on the other hand, unites people. A retreat director will have a better chance of connecting with the group if he or she touches common experience.

Avoid expressing controversial attitudes.

It's the director's responsibility to objectively handle controversy that may come up. However, controversy should not originate with the retreat director. Revealing controversial attitudes early on can evoke irritation in retreatants and may prevent them from hearing what the director has to say. This is not to say the director needs to be too vigilant in quashing any participant who dares to express controversy. Rather, the director validates what each retreatant says, controversial or not, but does not allow the controversy to take over the retreat.

In a family retreat, for example, parents may express discontent with the leadership of their church or with the lack of members' loyalty to church leadership. Sometimes a simple "I hear your concern. Thanks for sharing," from the director is the best response, especially if the comments wander from the focus of the retreat.

Notes
1. Thomas Keating, *Open Mind, Open Heart* (Rockport, Mass.: Element, Inc., 1992), 127-132.
2. Karl Pfeifer and Janeen Manternach, *This Is Our Faith, Teacher's Edition* (Parsippany, N.J.: Silver Burdett and Ginn, 1998), 368-369.
3. Dolores Curran, *Working With Parents* (Circle Pines, Minn.: American Guidance Service, 1989), 41-59.

What We Do and Why We Do It

2

Environment

"There are many rooms in my Father's house" (Jn. 14:2a).

Environment is a broad term used to describe the setting of the retreat. What children perceive on an emotional level about their retreat experience will stay with them; the aesthetics of the environment contribute to their impression. One of our teenagers, who started making retreats at age four, remembers climbing on a tractor at the rural retreat house. Another remembers how the singing echoed in the big, tall gathering room there. Adults, too, remember holidays and other special celebrations for their festivity, color, and warm ambience. All of these qualities come from the environment.

The setting of a children's retreat should be distinct from their normal classroom environment. A different meeting place is ideal, but if space is limited, the appearance of the classroom can be transformed by rearranging desks or adding simple decorations which reflect the theme of the retreat. For example, for the Good Friends retreat, where the children will spend part of their prayer time with Jesus in a fishing scene, a bulletin board could be posted with fish bearing each child's name, then covered with clear or blue plastic wrap to create the illusion of water. The desks can be moved aside to provide empty space, or chairs or desks can be arranged to approximate a large fishing boat. Children seven to ten have the gift of imagination to enhance their environment.

During the initial gathering time, and again at the closing, when all children and adults gather in one room, we set up an attractive focal point with articles reflecting the theme. This focal point should be dignified, yet appealing to children, holding such items as a Bible, a picture of Jesus, and toys and other props familiar to children, which will later be recognized as reflections of Jesus. Retreat directors are always encouraged to modify to their own tastes.

Nametags and Introductions

"I have called you by name: now you belong to me" (Isa. 43:1b).

In our classrooms, we've seen time and again how positively children respond when we use their names. In his prophetic message from God, Isaiah reminds us how sacred our names are. A fourth-grader once walked into his first day of school with a demeanor carried over from the year before, where he had felt rejection and ridicule from classmates. Shoulders slumped, eyes down, Houston slid into his desk where he hoped he could remain anonymous at best. As he was working, his teacher, unaware of his past, stooped down next to him and whispered, "Houston. That is the coolest name." Miracles didn't happen that day, but Houston looked into the teacher's eyes, smiled, and for a moment the two were bonded.

So it is with young retreatants. Because they are precious to God, God has called them by name. So must we—at every opportunity. For some, this may be one of the few times they hear their name spoken tenderly. For others, it may be the opening to an understanding of how interested Jesus really is in them, reflected by our genuine interest in them. For most, though, our calling them by name—right off their nametags—is one more affirmation of their uniqueness.

Gathering Time

"Whenever two or three of you come together in my name, I am there with you" (Mt. 18:20).

The gathering time lasts approximately twenty minutes and provides an opportunity to present the focus of the retreat to all retreatants at once. Children and adults join in song, then engage in a presentation that revolves around the theme of the retreat. The idea that we are all special friends of Jesus underlies the gathering and, bonded in this friendship, we trust in faith that Jesus is there.

Children's Activities

So Jesus called the children over to him and said, "Let the children come to me!" (Lk. 18:16a).

We know through faith that our lives abound with the presence and action of God. Elizabeth Barrett Browning wrote, "Earth is crammed with heaven, and every common bush afire with God." In nurturing spirituality in children, we try to fan the flame that's already there: their seemingly natural ability to see the extraordinary in the ordinary. This is not a complicated task, but rather a matter of consistent guidance on the part of adults. When children turn their minds and hearts to God, they're in prayer. We bring our children to Jesus, therefore, by heightening their awareness of how crammed their lives are with the rich friendship of Jesus in the activities they love—art, story, and imaginative play. *Every activity in a children's retreat is prayer.*

Souvenir

The souvenir is an art activity designed to serve as a reminder of the children's encounter with Jesus, and of the potential for continued deepening of this friendship after they return home. While the children are constructing the craft, the adult leader facilitates dialogue about the reality of the theme statements in the children's lives. To whatever extent the children are able to make this connection themselves, therein lies its power. For example, in the Good Friends retreat, the director might elicit from children times when they felt hope despite a bad situation, times when someone helped them or showed them friendship when they were having a hard time, and times when they showed friendship to someone who was having difficulty. In combination with their reflection on how Jesus would act in these same situations, the children are actually restating the three-fold focus of the retreat:

▲ Through everything that happens in our life, good or bad, Jesus is there.

▲ We are a presence of God's love to the people in our lives.

▲ By being good friends with others, we become better friends with Jesus.

Because the time period is limited to twenty minutes, and because the sharing is an important aspect of the souvenir prayer experience, the adult retreat team might consider simplifying the activity by preparing some of the craft ahead of time.

Story

We choose each story based on its relevance to the three-fold theme of a particular retreat. All of the retreats are based on the spirituality stated in the focus, and the story must remain true to that. If another book seems appropriate, we appeal to the director to weave the retreat theme throughout the story.

As with story time at home, the atmosphere should be relaxed and intimate. At one retreat, the director chose to sit in a big overstuffed chair, with the children at her feet, creating the image of well-known paintings where Jesus is surrounded by children. The children are in prayer as they listen to the story and examine in their hearts how the main character is like Jesus and how they, in turn, share those Christ-like qualities.

Prayer

The third prayer experience involves using the imagination to enter into union with Jesus. Children have responded well to our use of the term "heart room" as explained by Mary Terese Donze, ASC, in her book, *In My Heart Room.*[1] In this prayer form, we ask the children to imagine a room deep inside themselves. Jesus lives there, we tell them, and they can go there to be with Jesus whenever they want. It's in the "heart room" that we help the children visualize their friend Jesus, listen to him, speak to him, and sit with him in silence. Donze gives the following instruction for leading the children into their "heart rooms":

"Before giving directions to the children, make sure they are comfortably seated. If the prayer session is being held in the home or in an area of the school that is carpeted, the children may sit (not lie) comfortably on the floor.

"Help the children relax by taking them through a few breathing exercises. Direct them to breathe deeply and slowly (and silently) through the nose, in and out several times.

"If this is the children's first experience with this type of prayer, be sure they have been prepared beforehand by some short discussion of what they are going to do. Be brief. It is sufficient that the children realize they are praying and that it is a time of quiet.

"After the children have been prepared, begin the instructions. If you are standing, do not move from place to place as you read. Use a calm, quiet tone that is audible without being loud. Try to read as if you were speaking. Appeal to their hearts, but avoid the dramatic. State the direction in a simple, sincere way, keeping in mind your desire to lead the children to God through this prayer. Pause between sentences where the thought suggests a pause, but avoid prolonged silences. Move through the prayer with...deliberateness.

"Finally, begin well. Approach each prayer session asking God to bless you and the children you are trying to lead to [God]."

Some children may be familiar with the heart room prayer after having made several retreats for young children. For others, it will be unfamiliar and, perhaps, awkward. The most common barrier to being open to this type of prayer, we've found, is seven- to ten-year-olds' self-consciousness about keeping their eyes closed. Therefore, we assure them no one will be watching them, and that the adult director will keep her eyes open to make sure of this.

Snack
Seven- to ten-year-olds can have hefty appetites. Therefore, we provide a snack midway through the retreat to satisfy their physical needs. But the snack carries spiritual significance as well. Many in the Scriptures shared intimate times with Jesus at table. Indeed, our concept of Eucharist is rooted in this communion with each other, in this case, in the casual setting of a snack table.

Parent Sessions
"Anyone who hears and obeys these teachings of mine is like a wise person who built a house on solid rock... it did not fall, because it was built on solid rock" (Mt. 7:24, 25b).

Parents will be invited to some retreats for seven- to ten-year-olds and to family retreats. Our desire is to empower parents to be their children's primary religious educators with a solid theological foundation. This sixty-minute session, led by one of the retreat directors, embodies five elements:

1. overview
2. group introductions
3. explanation of children's activities
4. prayer
5. presentation

Overview

As the parents gather together for their session, we take care to emphasize why they are here. They've been invited to share a spiritual experience with their children as fellow retreatants. The parent talk, we explain, is an opportunity to meet with parents who have similar values and goals for their children, and in sharing God's word, to construct the metaphorical house on rock. Later they'll regroup with their children to share their own experience and to listen to their children's perceptions of friendship with Jesus gained in the prayer activities of the retreat.

Group Introductions

We invite the adults to introduce themselves, and in so doing, to answer a question. Their responses to the question have the effect of touching each other's common experience. The following questions have successfully elicited sharing at our retreats.

Choose one question per retreat:
▲ What do you most long for from God?
▲ What do you most want for your child?
▲ What specific help do you need to be more at ease sharing faith with your children?
▲ What's the most important thing about God that you want to communicate to your child?
▲ Share something your child has said about Jesus.
▲ Whom/what does your child remind you of?
▲ Why did you name your child as you did?
▲ What do you like most about seven- to ten-year-olds? least?
▲ Share something your child taught you about the love/goodness/wisdom of God.

Explanation of Children's Activities

We spend a few minutes explaining the format of the children's activities so that parents will be aware of the spirituality of their children's experiences. The children will have four twenty-minute sessions:

1. souvenir   2. story   3. prayer   4. snack

Prayer

We teach the parents the Heart Room Prayer following the guidelines outlined in Mary Terese Donze's *In My Heart Room*, and reproduced in this book on page 213.

Presentation

With the exception of the Eucharist and Reconciliation talks, the presentations are not tied to the themes of the retreats, so any talk can fit any retreat. The talks are founded on basic spiritual and theological truths which will enrich the parents' spirituality at the same time as it equips them with a foundation for sharing faith with their children. Each presentation is written in outline form so the director can flesh out the basic information with personal anecdotes, insights, and delivery style.

Adult-Child Sharing

The purpose of the sharing time is to discuss each person's retreat experience. As adult role models of faith to the children, the team leaders can effectively facilitate adult-child sharing following the children's activities if parents are not present. Questions to promote discussion are listed on page 214.

In addition, children might enjoy creating songs to tunes they already know, and sharing them with each other during the retreat closing. We provide a sample song for each retreat, but songwriting with the help of the adult facilitator can be a creative experience for both parties, as well as a bonding one. The songs should reflect the theme of the retreat.

At retreats where parents are present, families have the rich opportunity to share faith during this time. Many parents are inexperienced at sharing faith with their children, and in fact find it uncomfortable. We've found more success with parent-child sharing time when we give each parent a copy of questions they can ask their children, page 214.

Letters to the Family

When parents are not present at the retreat, we provide a letter to send home which encourages parent participation in extending the retreat. The letter informs parents of the focus of the retreat and the content of each activity, and invites parents to engage in specific spiritual experiences with their children. The family activities are a response to parents who requested a structure for sharing faith. They provide the added benefit of one-on-one time between parent and child. We inform the children of the letter they'll take home and instill enthusiasm for sharing their retreat with their parents.

Closing

"I hope that as you become stronger in your faith, we will be able to reach many more of the people around you" (2 Cor. 10:15).

The closing is brief, but summarizes what the retreatants have experienced, reaffirming their friendship with Jesus. This can take the form of eliciting answers to questions, giving a three- or four-sentence statement, singing songs, praying, or a combination of these.

At the end of each retreat in this book, we include a closing litany, which reinforces the theme of the retreat. In addition, if the children's attention is still strong, this is a wonderful opportunity for the children to share the songs they composed during the adult-child sharing. Remember, though, to keep it brief. The children are ready to go home. We send them with increased faith and with the hope that their influence will be large in their home and school communities.

Child Care

"Then Jesus said, 'Let's go to a place where we can be alone and get some rest'" (Mk. 6:31a).

We've found that our retreats draw greater numbers when we offer child care for younger siblings. In a family retreat, of course, three- to six-year-olds will be among the retreatants. But if the retreat is specifically for seven- to ten-year-olds and their parents, all younger siblings should be entertained with activities of their own apart from older retreatants. Some parishes provide a more loosely structured version of the art, story, and prayer activities for the younger children. It would be powerful to post the three-fold retreat theme on the wall of the child care facility so the provider could repeat the statements throughout the morning. Child care provides time away for parents and a special focus on the retreatants of the day. It's always helpful to families to provide child care if facilities permit.

Note
1. Mary Terese Donze, *In My Heart Room* (Liguori, Mo.: Liguori Publications, 1982), 7.

3 Parent-Child Retreats

Schedule

We offer two types of retreats: a daytime experience and an evening retreat. We follow these schedules:

Daytime Retreat

9:15 am	Retreatants Arrive (put on nametags, greet each other and the retreat team)
9:30-9:45	Introduction and Focus
9:45-10:45	Parents' Session (if parents are present)
9:45-10:45	Children's Activities
10:45-11:00	Snack
11:00-11:20	Adult-Child Sharing
11:20-11:30	Closing
11:30	Group Lunch (optional)

Evening Retreat

5:15-6:15 pm	Potluck Dinner (optional)
6:30-6:45	Introduction and Focus
6:45-7:45	Parents' Session (if parents are present)
6:45-7:45	Children's Activities
7:45-8:00	Snack
8:00-8:20	Adult-Child Sharing
8:20-8:30	Closing

1-Eucharist Retreat

(1 Corinthians 12:4-31)

If giving a family retreat that includes three- to six-year-olds, coordinate with the retreat entitled "Thanksgiving" from *Parent-Child Retreats: Spiritual Experiences for Children Ages 3-6 and Their Parents* (Living the Good News, 1997).

Focus

Eucharist is our coming together as a community to "give thanks" to our loving God in Jesus. In the Eucharist, Jesus living and present gives himself to us under the appearance of bread and wine. In receiving him we become one with him and with all believers. The unity and connectedness of all believers weaves its way through this retreat.

As children prepare for first Eucharist, their significant adults' own faith in Jesus and understanding of the Eucharist is vital to the children's growth in faith that

Jesus is present in the Eucharist. The power of this retreat increases when the parents share in their children's sacramental preparation through this experience of friendship and communion with Jesus. Jesus himself shared his last supper with his best friends, modeling for us the significance of our oneness with Jesus and with each other in Eucharist.

Children's faith in the mystery of the real presence of Jesus under the signs of bread and wine is supported by the experience of communion with those they love at meal time. This "union with" friends, family, and strangers flows out of the oneness we have with Jesus and with each other in Eucharist. Being a presence of God's love to each other in ways that are specific to our personality and state in life is our role as a member of the Body of Christ.

The focus of the retreat can be summarized in these statements:
▲ When we receive the eucharist, we receive Jesus under the appearance of bread and wine. We become united with Jesus, and he with us.
▲ Because we are united with Jesus, we see Jesus in each other.
▲ Each of us is a message of love from God to everyone else.
▲ When we are with each other in love we are the Body of Christ.

Preparations Before the Retreat

1. Meet as a team to pray, read, discuss, understand, and interiorize the focus and scriptural basis for the retreat.
2. Discern which team members will be responsible for the gathering presentation, each of the three children's activities, and the adult retreat section, if there is one.
3. If this is to be a family retreat or a retreat for sacramental preparation, choose "Eucharist" from the section entitled Outlines for Parent Sessions (p. 152). If parents will not be present, prepare a letter to send home for parent-child follow-up enrichment (p. 185).
4. Divide preparation responsibilities. Use the gifts of the community to lighten the load. Parents, teenagers, school children, and senior citizens can all help prepare.

Make nametags in three colors.

Collect materials for the environment.
▲ Bible
▲ picture of Jesus

▲ sample souvenir

▲ book for story session

▲ chalice

▲ paten

▲ ciborium

Prepare the retreat souvenir (p. 24).

First, gather materials for each retreatant:

▲ large grocery sacks

▲ scissors

▲ pencil

▲ 3" x 12" strips cut from construction paper

▲ four-inch red hearts cut from construction paper

For retreatants to share:

▲ markers

▲ glue (one for every two children)

▲ gummed stars or stickers and objects to glue on: crepe paper streamers, bits of wallpaper or gift wrap, sequins/beads, pre-cut construction paper shapes

Second, do the advance preparation.

1. Write ideas from the Body of Christ list (p. 195) on large poster board or chalkboard for children to refer to when they write on their 3" x 12" strips.
2. Cut out the neck and armholes for each retreatant's vest by following the picture guide (p. 24-25) and trim the front with slightly curved lines as shown.
3. Complete one sample vest for demonstration.

Locate the story.

Obtain *Old Turtle* by Douglas Wood (Duluth, Minn.: Pfifer-Hamilton Publishers, 1992).

If unable to locate the first literature choice of literature, substitute *Everybody Cooks Rice* by Norah Dooley (New York: Scholastic, 1992).

Prepare for the gathering presentation.

Cut a 12" diameter circle from sturdy white paper or poster board. In large letters, write "Communion" on one side and "Being With" on the other side. Gather packaging from familiar foods, such as empty cans of soup or vegetables, empty boxes of cereal or macaroni and cheese.

Become familiar with the heart room prayer (p. 28).

Purchase groceries and prepare the snack.

▲ pizza

or

▲ English muffins or bagels, pizza sauce, and cheese

▲ soft drinks or fruit juice

Duplicate the Adult-Child Sharing Form (p. 214) or letter to parents (p. 185).

Preparations the Day of the Retreat

1. Gather as a team and pray.
2. Set out nametags and safety pins or tape *(warning: no straight pins or strings).* Have exactly as many nametags as retreatants, and equal numbers of nametags for each color group.
3. Have each retreat team member wear a different colored nametag. This will later help the children divide into groups for their activities.
4. On top of a piano or table, create the environment in the gathering room with an arrangement of familiar products and packaging from local eating places. Include the book that will be read during the retreat, a sample of the souvenir the children will make, a picture of Jesus, a Bible, a chalice, ciborium, and paten.
5. Gather all the materials for the retreat souvenir and set out on tables in the room that will be used for this activity.
6. Spread out so that at least one team member is greeting the retreatants as they arrive, one is bringing retreatants (and parents) to the gathering room, one is waiting in the gathering room, and one is directing parents and younger siblings to the nursery.
7. Begin the retreat by warmly greeting the retreatants, then introducing the team members.

Gathering Presentation

How many of you have heard the word "Eucharist"?—raise your hands. Eucharist means the great sacrament when the Risen Jesus gives himself to all believers under the appearance of bread and wine. We often speak of receiving Jesus in the Eucharist as receiving communion when we are united with him and all other believers.

Jesus showed us how to make an ordinary supper into something special. When he and his friends were at supper together, he changed an ordinary meal into Eucharist. At that last supper with his friends, Jesus broke some bread apart and gave it to them. He said, "This is my body, which I am going to give for you. Do this in memory of me." Each time we receive the Eucharist, we receive what looks like bread but is Jesus under the appearance of bread and wine. We believe the bread is Jesus because he said, *"I am the bread that gives life! I am that bread from heaven! Everyone who eats it will live forever. My flesh is the life-giving bread that I give to the people of this world"* (Jn. 6:48, 51).[1]

Eucharist started with Jesus and his friends at the last supper, celebrating a special Jewish feast called Passover. At the end of the meal, Jesus took bread and wine and blessed them, saying, *"This is my body, which is given for you"* (Lk. 22:19). Whenever we eat this bread and drink this cup, Jesus is with us. At Eucharist, when we are all together, we become one with Jesus and also with one another. We are the people of God.

Think about meal time. *(Point to the props on the table: packaging from familiar eating places and familiar products.)* This is all ordinary stuff. But what makes it better than just a meal is that we're with people we really love.

Now listen to this: *Wherever there is love, Jesus is there.*

I'd like to hear you say that. *Wherever there is love, Jesus is there. (Allow time for the children to repeat.)*

That's a very important message. Because Jesus gave himself to us in Eucharist, we are united with Jesus and with each other. So *wherever there is love, Jesus is there.*

We receive communion on Sunday because it unites us to Jesus and all the people of God. Another way of saying "the people of God" is "the Body of Christ." St. Paul used this phrase to speak of our oneness with Christ. He said, *"the body of Christ has many different parts, just as any other body does....But God's Spirit baptized each of us and made us part of the body of Christ"* (1 Cor. 12:12-13).

Do you see how different all of us are? Some of us are adults, some are children. We look different; we're different sizes. We're good at this, or good at that.

It's important in a body that the parts be different. We should be happy about that. Otherwise, the body wouldn't work right. It's also important that all the different parts of the body do what they're supposed to do, rather than something else. Eyes, for example, can't talk. And they shouldn't try to. Otherwise, what would do the seeing?

Let's do some pretending. I need five volunteers. Let's all sit in a circle and cover everything except our feet. We are nothing but feet now. No heads, mouths, or eyes. No hands. No arms. Just feet. Now, Jessica, with your feet, ask Jared to pass the spaghetti. Jared, pass the spaghetti to Jessica—with your feet, remember. You have no hands. Quevana, Tanya is feeling sad today. Why don't you give her a hug? With your feet, remember—you have no arms. Everyone! Listen! Do you hear that fire engine? Listen—with your feet, remember. Fred, would you please help Anthony tie his shoes? Thanks, Fred. Now, everyone, let's go back and sit with our parents. But remember—just your feet can go. That's all you have! *(Allow time for the children to return to their seats.)*

Gosh! Being a body with all feet caused some problems, didn't it? The Body of Christ could have some problems, too, if all of us were the same. What if we were all laughers? Or all criers? What if we were all talkers? Or all shy? What if we all wanted to be the helpers? What if we didn't have anybody to help? What if we all wanted to be helped? What if there were no one to help us? Being the body of Christ means we are united with Jesus and with each other in Eucharist, all different, but all valuable.

We have some fun activities to do now. Let me show you what we'll be doing. *(Show the children the souvenir and story, and tell them they'll also be talking to Jesus.)*

Now look at the color of your nametag. *(Have the children leave the room with the team leader who has the same colored nametag.)*

Children's Activities

The following three children's activities run simultaneously, and the children rotate through them until they've been to all three.

Activity 1: Art as Prayer—Retreat Souvenir

The retreatants will make Body of Christ Grocery Bag Vests. As members of the Body of Christ, the children will express their unity with each other as they all create the same product, their uniqueness in the art they create, and connectedness with the larger community as they reflect on various members of the Body of Christ.

As the children fashion their vests, talk about the focus of the retreat (p.20).

Gather participants around the materials table to create Body of Christ vests:

1. Participants write their names in pencil inside the vests

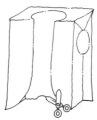

where they will not be seen, but can be identified when they go home.

2. Retreat director and children brainstorm who is in the Body of Christ, using the prepared list (p. 195) as a starter, if needed.

3. Children select one group of people within the Body of Christ they would like to represent artistically on their vests. They write those words on the back side of their vest. (*Examples: parents, community workers, friends, relatives, teachers.*)

4. The adult leader reinforces the variety of people in the Body of Christ by reading the labels as students work. "Government workers are in the Body of Christ. Babysitters are in the Body of Christ. People in nursing homes are in the Body of Christ, etc..."

5. Participants complete their vests by gluing the four-inch heart cut-out near the front opening as a pocket. They use markers and glue-ons to decorate the vest surfaces.

6. Retreatants can wear their vests throughout the retreat. The vests will become part of the final celebration at the closing prayer gathering.

7. As follow-up at home, parents and children will add the words "We see God in each other."

Announce to the children: It's almost time to move to your next prayer session. Please help me get ready for the next group by setting up the table the way it was when you arrived. (*To the final group, give directions about how to put supplies away.*)

Activity 2: Story as Prayer

Story: *Old Turtle* by Douglas Wood (Duluth, Minn.: Pfifer-Hamilton Publishers, 1992)

As the children listen to and discuss the literature, talk about the focus of the retreat (p.20).

Greet the children.

(*As retreatants enter the room, designate a space where they can put their belongings, then invite them to sit in a place where they can see the pictures in the book.*)

Raise your hand if you've heard this story before. Wonderful. If you have, let's not tell the others what happens so they can enjoy their experience, too.

This is a time of prayer. Let's get ready to listen to what God wants us to hear in this story. Are you in a comfortable position? Let's all take a deep breath and let it out a little at a time.

Introduce the story.

This is the story of how the creatures of the earth argued among themselves about who or what God is. Some said God is gentle, others, powerful. Some argued that God is above all things. Some believed God is within all things.

In this story, Old Turtle says there will soon be a strange and wonderful new family of beings in the world—a reminder of all that God is. These people will be a message of love from God to the earth and a prayer from the earth back to God. Listen for the part where Old Turtle smiles and so does God. God's voice comes from the mountain, the ocean, the stone, the breeze, and the star. We'll talk about that part after we finish the book.

Read the story, taking ample time to show the pictures.

(Using voice intonations, pauses, and a prayerful sense of awe, read the book aloud. Allow time for children to be touched by the words as well as the illustrations. At the conclusion, close the book gently and allow a moment of "think time.")

Talk about the story.

▲ That was quite a story. What was happening early in the book? *(The creatures were arguing about who God is.)*

▲ As it got louder, something unusual happened: Old Turtle spoke up. Why was that unusual? *(He hardly ever said anything.)*

▲ Old Turtle said the people would be a message of love from God to the earth. Do you know someone else God sent to be a message of love to the earth? *(Jesus.)*

▲ Old Turtle said that the people were supposed to be a prayer to God. How do we know they forgot? *(They argued and hurt one another as well as the earth.)*

▲ Why do you think Old Turtle and God smiled in the end? *(They were pleased because the creatures were seeing God in one another. They were united now, rather than divided.)*

▲ Was there anything in this book that reminded you of the People of God? *(Once the creatures had a new vision that they were a message of God's love to each other, they were united with God and with each other.)*

26

▲ Which character reminded you of Jesus? *(Affirm all answers. Encourage children to elaborate by asking for more information with questions like, "What was it about that character that made you think of Jesus?" or "Can you say more?")*

▲ What did you like about this book? What didn't you like?

(Hold up the book with the cover facing the children.) When you're telling your family about the book you read during the retreat today, remember this title. Let's say it together: *Old Turtle.*

Announce to the children: Now it's time to move to the next retreat session. Be sure to take any of your belongings with you on your way out. Let's walk together.

Alternate Story

If the first choice of literature for this session is unavailable, substitute *Everybody Cooks Rice* by Norah Dooley (Scholastic: New York, 1992) and change the letter to parents.

Introduction:

Carrie, of Italian descent, searched for her brother Anthony in the neighborhood among the neighbors from Barbados, Puerto Rico, Vietnam, India, China, and Haiti. In each household at suppertime she found a similarity—they all cooked rice. Each family had its own tradition around eating and seasoning it, but it was rice just the same. In this diverse Body of Christ that welcomed Carrie into their homes, God was present in the love between generations of family members as well as in their care for Carrie's brother Anthony.

Anthony and Carrie had both participated in Eucharist—Thanksgiving—all over their neighborhood while they ate a few bites with other families and heard God's message of love in each person they met. All were united with Jesus and with each other.

Reading:

(Throughout the story, point out who is serving the other members of the family: Carrie's mom is cooking dinner; Mr. and Mrs. D. are sharing dinner with their grandchildren; Fendra and Tito Diaz are cooking for their working mom; Tam is taking a turn cooking for the Tran family; Rajit is carrying dinner to his parent in a tiffin carrier; Mrs. Hua and Mrs. Bleu are adding their special ingredients for their families.)

Discussion:

▲ Who has God sent to your neighborhood to love you, someone who is *not* in your immediate family? *(Invite each retreatant to respond.)*

▲ Who in this story was like Jesus? *(Possible responses: All the people noted above who were serving others; Carrie looking for Anthony like Jesus looking for the lost sheep; other ideas provided by the children.)*

▲ Whom do you know in the People of God that looks different from your family? *(Listen to as many comparisons as time will allow, verbally reinforcing with the words "And they're in the Body of Christ" a few times throughout the listing process.)*

Activity 3: The Heart Room Prayer

Weave the focus of the retreat throughout the children's experience of the heart room prayer.

(Greet the children as they arrive, then invite them to sit in a circle with you. Be sure the circle is large enough that there is room between the children and they don't touch each other. Welcome the children.)

Guess what? We've been invited to a friend's house for pizza today. We have to drive there in our car. Wanna go? There's going to be a surprise guest with us. Our friend has invited Jesus to have pizza with us. Are you ready? Let's go! *(Inform the children that they're not actually going to eat pizza during the prayer time, but that they will when they gather for snack.)*

Check in your pocket. Do you have your car key? Great. Look behind you for any traffic. When it's clear unlock the car and get in. Be sure to pull the seatbelt in place. There. Oh, I noticed the back window is open. Would you reach back and close it, please, Molly? *(Volunteer makes the motion of turning around, reaching for the window handle.)* Thanks.

Now, if there are no cars coming turn on the ignition and let the car warm up for a second. *(Pause.)*

Okay, let's go. Be sure there are no cars coming in our lane. Did you check the rear-view mirror? Good. Better get in the other lane. We have to put our blinker on at the end of the block.... Okay, put on your left blinker. The coast is clear. Turn left here. *(Take a few steps, turning to the left.)* I always hate to do this street when the weather's bad—it's so steep. Give it a little more gas. Up we go. *(Take a few steps with exaggerated exertion, the children following.)*

So far, so good. Oh, no! Step on the brake! *(Make screeching sounds.)* It's a dog! Phew! That was close. Now, at the end of the block we turn right. *(Take a few steps, turning to the right.)* You're great drivers. I feel safe with you.

Oh, there's the house. We're lucky. Plenty of parking places in front. Here we are. Turn off the ignition. Now let's all get out.

(Begin to slow down the pace, lowering the voice.)

Luke, would you ring the doorbell for us? Here they come. I love coming here for dinner. Let's go inside. Ooh... the table is all set and the house smells great. *(Take a deep breath.)* Shall we sit down? *(Place a tablecloth on the floor and instruct the children to sit around it.)*

I'm glad to see an empty seat there between Joe and Caitlin. We have a special guest joining us today, someone who likes pizza as much as we do. Remember that I told you our friend invited Jesus to join us? Today we're going to visit with Jesus, to pray with Jesus as our dinner guest.

I'd like to show you a way you can pray and talk with Jesus. It's important to know, though, that Jesus isn't somewhere far away. Jesus lives within each one of us, in a place deep inside. I call this place the heart room. Your heart room is a place where it's quiet, where you can go anytime you want to and place yourself in the presence of Jesus, your friend.

It helps me to close my eyes and tune out any sounds. Let's all close our eyes. Don't worry that you'll be the only one. I'll keep my own eyes open to make sure it's safe for everyone. All of us have our eyes closed so we won't be distracted.

I'll lead you now through some helps for praying in our heart room. First, take a deep breath to help you relax. Fine. Let's take another deep breath. We all have our eyes closed. As I lead you through this type of prayer please use my suggestions to make pictures in your mind.

We're all sitting around the table. *(Pause.)* Someone just walked into the room, our heart room. It's Jesus. *(Pause.)* What does he look like? What color is his hair? Is it curly? Straight? Long? Short? *(Pause.)* Now look at his face. Is he smiling? How does he look at you? *(Pause.)* When you look at his face do you feel peaceful, happy? What are your feelings when you look at Jesus' face? How is Jesus dressed? What color is his skin?

Jesus sits down next to you. *(Pause.)* Make yourself comfortable next to Jesus. He's there only for you. What would you like to say to Jesus? In our heart room, we don't have to worry that we might say the wrong thing or that Jesus might not understand us. Knowing we're with such an incredibly good friend, let's take a minute to talk with Jesus right now. I'll stop for a short time and you can tell Jesus whatever you would like. Jesus might also want to say something to you. So listen...

(Wait 60 seconds.)

It's time to go now. Say goodbye to Jesus in whatever way you'd like. Wave, hug him, or say some simple words. *(Pause.)* Tell Jesus you'll come back to your heart room again. *(Pause.)* Now imagine yourself walking back to our room here. *(Pause.)*

When you're ready, please open your eyes.

Sometimes it helps to look back on what happened in prayer in our heart rooms. How did you feel when you were in your heart room? Did you have an easy time talking to Jesus? Do you believe he heard you? Did Jesus say anything to you? Sometimes we hear Jesus and sometimes we don't. That's natural. *(Allow children time to share.)*

Now that you've had a chance to talk to Jesus in your heart room, you can do this anytime you want. There's no place off-limits for talking to Jesus, no time that's too early or too late. You can repeat this prayer anytime you feel you'd like to talk to Jesus. The heart room has been a good, peaceful place, hasn't it?

This table was so inviting. We ate ordinary food, but it was special this time: Jesus was with us. Because Jesus comes to each of us in Eucharist under the signs of bread and wine, we are united to Jesus, and we bring Jesus to the meals we share with others.

We shared a lot and now it's time to go. Stand up. Do you have your keys ready? Let's go get in the car. Follow me. We'll take the same route home. What a trip! The pizza was delicious, and best of all, we had a chance to get to know Jesus in a new way.

Remember what we did here in our retreat. I hope you have many happy and prayerful times with Jesus in your heart room when you pray this way again.

Snack

pizza
soft drinks or fruit juice

Adult-Child Sharing Time

After the adult session, parents or adult retreat leaders join their children in the snack room to begin their sharing time. If weather permits, retreatants can go outside for a nature walk. If not, they might want to find a corner to sit in, take a walk through the church, spread out blankets throughout the room, or even create forts out of blankets to sit in for privacy. We allow approximately twenty minutes for adult-child sharing time, asking all participants to return to the gathering room at the allotted time for our closing.

The questions on p. 214 can facilitate adult-child sharing.

If time remains, parents or adult leaders can lead children in familiar Eucharist hymns or help children compose a song to a familiar tune, using the focus of the retreat.

For example:
(To the tune of Kum-ba-yah)

> Bread and wine he took, bread and wine.
> Bread and wine he shared, bread and wine.
> Bread and wine he gave, bread and wine.
> Jesus gave us bread and wine.
> It is now his body and his blood.
> It is now his body and his blood.
> It is now his body and his blood.
> Since he gave us bread and wine.
> You and I receive Jesus' life.
> You and I can share Jesus' love.
> You and I can share Jesus' love.
> Since he gave us bread and wine.

(To accommodate children who are not auditory learners, print the lyrics of each song on a large poster board and display.)

Closing Prayer

The children can close with song, singing familiar Eucharistic hymns or teaching each other the lyrics their group composed earlier. Following the prayer of joyful song, an adult facilitator leads the children in the following litany:

> *Adult:* I invite all of you to join me in prayer. First, I'll say something to God for all of us. Then you say, "We're united with you in Eucharist, Jesus."

Adult:	Jesus, when we receive the Eucharist, we receive you under the appearance of bread and wine.
Children:	We're united with you in Eucharist, Jesus.
Adult:	Jesus, when we receive Eucharist, we are united with you and you with us.
Children:	We're united with you in Eucharist, Jesus.
Adult:	Jesus, because we are united with you, we see God in each other.
Children:	We're united with you in Eucharist, Jesus.
Adult:	Jesus, because you are united with us, each of us is a message of love from God to everyone else.
Children:	We're united with you in Eucharist, Jesus.
Adult:	Jesus, when we are with each other in love we are the Body of Christ.
Children:	We're united with you in Eucharist, Jesus.

Invite children to join hands and say the Our Father.

Note

1. Christiane Brusselmans and Brian A. Haggerty, *We Celebrate the Eucharist: Program Director's Manual* (Morristown, N.J.: Silver Burdett and Ginn, 1984), 170.

2-Reconciliation Retreat

(Matthew 18:10-14; Luke 23:34)

If giving a family retreat that includes three- to six-year-olds, coordinate with the retreat entitled "Kite" from *Parent-Child Retreats: Spiritual Experiences for Children Ages 3-6 and Their Parents* (Living the Good News, 1997).

Focus

Children have learned from early on the need to say "I'm sorry" and "I forgive you." One of the endless tasks of parents is to train children to say such phrases with sincerity. "Sorry," said with a punch, or "That's okay, but..." are favorite techniques children use to fulfill their obligation without letting go of their anger towards the offender. Many adults "forgive" in the same way.

We've learned, however, that when we hang onto anger, the anger turns inward, often resulting in physical, emotional, and spiritual disorders. Our model for genuine forgiveness is a loving, merciful God.

The sacrament of Reconciliation offers us the opportunity to experience genuine forgiveness from this loving God, who forgives us without hesitation. In the sacrament of Reconciliation, we recognize both our sinfulness and God's abundant forgiveness. The forgiveness we receive from God brings us back into a loving relationship where we feel more peaceful, better about ourselves, and desiring to live a more loving life again. Because God forgives us in this way, we try to forgive others, too—with sincerity, with love, and without hesitation, resentment, or revenge.

Children can look to their friend Jesus, whose life was replete with opportunities to forgive, as a model of God's forgiveness. He was frequently the target of mocking and doubting during his public ministry. Two of his closest friends betrayed him. But perhaps the most difficult example Jesus provided us was his forgiveness of his tormentors and persecutors as he died on the cross. His words, "Father, forgive them; they do not know what they are doing," are haunting in light of the small transgressions we ourselves fail to forgive on a daily basis. This is not a condemnation, but a statement of God's endless mercy and forgiveness at work in his son, Jesus. God is willing to be the source of forgiveness in us, too, as we struggle with our human nature which resists the difficult task of forgiving.

The focus of the retreat can be summarized in four statements:
▲ Because God made us, we are good. However, we may do bad things.
▲ In the sacrament of Reconciliation, we are reunited with God and each other.
▲ When God forgives us, God brings us back into a loving relationship where we feel more peaceful, better about ourselves, and want to live a more loving life again.
▲ Because God forgives us endlessly in our sinfulness, we learn to forgive others in the same way.

Preparations Before the Retreat

1. Meet as a team to pray, read, discuss, understand, and interiorize the focus and scriptural basis for the retreat.

2. Discern which team members will be responsible for the gathering presentation, each of the three children's activities, and the adult retreat section, if there is one.

3. If this is to be a family retreat or a retreat for sacramental preparation, choose "Reconciliation" from the section entitled Outlines for Parent Sessions (p. 157). Additional parent retreats are available from *Parent-Child Retreats: Spiritual Experiences for Children Ages 3-6 and Their Parents* (Living the Good News, 1997). If parents will not be present, prepare a letter to send home for parent-child follow-up enrichment (p. 187).

4. Divide preparation responsibilities. Use the gifts of the community to lighten the load. Parents, teenagers, school children, and senior citizens can all help prepare.

Make nametags in three colors.

Collect materials for the environment.
▲ Bible
▲ picture of Jesus
▲ sample souvenir
▲ book for story session
▲ banner that says "I'm sorry—I forgive you"

Prepare the retreat souvenir (p. 39).
First, gather materials for each retreatant:
▲ standard size file folder, any color
▲ three gameboard masters (see pp. 197-199)
▲ clear contact paper 12" x 24" (or ability and personnel for quick lamination)
▲ scissors
▲ pencil
▲ paper fastener (brad)
▲ four different colored buttons
▲ sandwich size recloseable plastic bag
▲ large paper clip

For retreatants to share:
▲ glue (one for each two retreatants working in a group)
▲ colored pencils/fine tipped markers
▲ gummed stars or stickers
▲ masking tape
▲ drinking straw (one for every two)

Second, do the advance preparation:

1. Cut straws in half at a slant.
2. Attach plastic bag filled with four different colored buttons, 1/2 straw, and one paper fastener to three game masters and then to each file folder.
3. Complete one sample game for demonstration following directions on p. 40.

Locate the story.

Lilly's Purple Plastic Purse by Kevin Henkes (New York: Greenwillow Books, 1996). If unable to locate the first literature choice, substitute *The Conversation Club* by Diane Stanley (New York: Macmillan Publishing Company, 1990) and change the letter to parents.

Prepare for the gathering presentation.

Duplicate one Random Act of Forgiveness Award (p. 196) for each child re-treatant and an extra large one *(on poster board)* to present to Jesus during the gathering presentation.

Become familiar with the heart room prayer (p. 43).

Gather materials: 8 notecards, approximately 5" x 8"; 1 magic marker.

Purchase groceries and prepare the snack.

cookies and milk *(With frosting, write Sorry, or S, on half the cookies and Forgive, or F, on the rest.)*

Duplicate the Adult-Child Sharing Form (p. 214) or letter to parents (p. 187)

Preparations the Day of the Retreat

1. Gather as a team and pray.
2. Set out nametags and safety pins or tape *(warning: no straight pins or strings)*. Have exactly as many nametags as retreatants, and equal numbers of nametags for each color group.
3. Have each retreat team member wear a different colored nametag. This will later help the children divide into groups for their activities.
4. On top of a piano or table, create the environment in the gathering room with an arrangement that reflects the theme of the retreat. Include the book that will be read during the retreat, a sample of the souvenir the children will make, and a Bible.
5. Gather all the materials for the retreat souvenir and set out on tables in the room that will be used for this activity.
6. Spread out so that at least one team member is greeting the retreatants as they

arrive, one is bringing retreatants (and parents) to the gathering room, one is waiting in the gathering room, and one is directing parents and younger siblings to the nursery.

7. Begin the retreat by warmly greeting the retreatants, then introducing the team members.

Gathering Presentation

(Choose participants to act out this story. Coach the children ahead of time or write the dialogue on poster board for children to read. In order to guide the dialogue, the adult leader should play the part of Susan's mother.)

I'm glad you're here today. We're going to be doing some fun things together on our retreat. The best part, I think, is that in the middle of doing fun things we'll be learning something about Jesus and how much God loves us. You already know that God made each one of us and that because God made us, we are good. But have you noticed that sometimes we do bad things? I want to tell you a story about how someone who is good in God's eyes did something bad.

One day last week Susan came home from school and asked if she could go to Colleen's house to watch a movie with their group of friends. Susan's mom told her she could go but that it was very important that she be home by 5:30 because they were having company for dinner. Their neighbors, the Brownstones, were coming over for a barbecue to celebrate Dylan Brownstone's fifth birthday. Dylan adored her older friend Susan, and always wanted to spend time with her.

Susan, Colleen, and their friends were in the middle of the movie when Colleen suddenly interrupted. "Oh no! Susan, look! It's almost 6:00. Aren't you supposed to be home at 5:30?" Susan thought about her mother's orders, about her neighbor Dylan and Dylan's family, and about her friends and the movie they were watching. "Aw, don't worry," she finally said. "I'm going to stay with all of you and watch the end of this movie. I don't want to leave yet. This is more fun than a dumb old barbecue."

Well, you guessed it. Susan decided to stay, and when she did leave it was almost 8:00. As she was running home, Susan thought about how late it was. The lights in the kitchen were out and the food had been put away. As Susan came in the front door her little brother ran up and announced in a loud voice: "Oh-oh, Susan, you're really in big trouble. Mom is so mad at you." Susan didn't want to see her mom and dad. She felt terrible.

Her mom was furious. "Susan, we've been waiting for you. Look, it's already dark outside. I was so worried. No one answered the phone at Colleen's house. We were afraid you'd been hurt or that something happened to you." Her dad added, "Susan, we were worried. What took you so long?" Before Susan could answer, her mom told her how worried the neighbors had been. *(Children in the audience can murmur, "Where is Susan? Is she hurt? Is she coming home?")* "And Susan," her mom said, "little Dylan was so sad when you didn't come to celebrate her birthday."

Susan's mom tried to explain to Susan. "What you did was wrong. You hurt all of us. The neighbors were worried, your dad went out looking for you, and Dylan's feelings were hurt. We all wanted you to be at our dinner."

Susan felt sad. She had deliberately chosen to miss dinner and her young neighbor's birthday celebration. She sensed everyone's disappointment and felt separated from them. All she wanted was to be united with her family again, and to make things right with little Dylan. She was deeply sorry for the hurt she had caused others. "I'm sorry," she said through her tears.

Her mom looked at her and said softly, "What you did hurt all of us. It was wrong. I forgive you, Susan. Now I think you need some time with Jesus. Tell him you want to be reunited with him. Tell him you're sorry and he will forgive you right away. Jesus knows you're good because God made you." Susan did spend time with Jesus in prayer, then ran next door to apologize to the Brownstones and wish Dylan a happy birthday.

Now, can you tell us what Susan did that was bad? *(Listen to examples.)* What did Susan's mom say to Susan? *(Elicit a list of Mom's remarks.)* Is there anything in that list that sounds like how God forgives us and helps us to be reunited with each other? *(Encourage answers.)*

This is what the sacrament of Reconciliation is like. Though we are good because God made us, we all do bad things at times. Yet when we are sorry and ask to be forgiven, we receive God's forgiveness immediately and endlessly. Just as Susan felt sad because she had separated herself from her family, her neighbors, and the young friend who adored her, sin makes us feel separated from God. When we talk about the sacrament of Reconciliation, we mean that we are once again reunited with God, which helps us feel better about ourselves and fills us with a desire to live a more loving life again.

Hey, I have an idea! Let's give Jesus an award to show how thankful we are that he forgives us just as soon as we ask for it. Look what I have. *(Hold up a Random Act of Forgiveness Award.)*

This is a Random Act of Forgiveness Award. It says, "This award is presented to you for forgiving me and for helping me feel more peaceful, better about myself, and more wanting to live a loving life again." Then I'll sign my name in the last space. What do you think? Should we write this award for Jesus, who always forgives us?

I have another idea. I think I'd like to give each of you a Random Act of Forgiveness Award, too. You forgave me as Jesus did. *(Have helpers hand out awards.)*

Hold on to these now. This is your award, but I have a suggestion: You could give this award to someone else when they forgive you for something. Then they could give the award to someone else, and that person could give it to someone else, and pretty soon we would notice how everybody is forgiving everybody else. Random Act of Forgiveness Awards would soon be all over our *(school, parish, town)*. Pretty soon we would all be forgiving each other just as Jesus does. Should we try it?

We have some fun activities to do now. Let me show you what we'll be doing. *(Show the children the souvenir and story, and tell them they'll also be talking to Jesus.)*

Now look at the color of your nametag. *(Have the children leave the room with the team leader who has the same colored nametag.)*

Children's Activities

The following three children's activities run simultaneously, and the children rotate through them until they've been to all three.

Activity 1: Art as Prayer—Retreat Souvenir

Retreatants will construct individual Reconciliation board games which they can play with a peace partner at home as a way to practice forgiving and being forgiven. As the children create their game board, talk to them about the focus of the retreat (p.34).

Gather participants around materials tables where they will construct a Reconciliation board game:

1. Participants write their names in pencil on the outside *back* of the file folder. This will be the only surface not used to construct the game.
2. Retreat leader quickly reviews the focus from the opening session.
3. Adult leader demonstrates a sample game board.

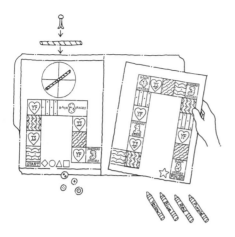 

4. Children glue the title page on the front cover of the file folder. *(If re-treatants have extra time, they can decorate the outside of the game.)*

5 Participants glue two sheets together on the center fold making sure they touch and are straight, and leaving a bit of a border around the outside edge.

6. Children let glue dry for about two minutes.

7. Retreatants choose four colors for the spinner and color in each section of the spinner circle with a different color.

8. Choosing one of those same four colors, children fill in the stripes on the first striped square of the gameboard. With a second color, they fill in the stripes of the next striped square; with a third color, the stripes of the third striped square; and with a fourth color, the stripes of the last striped square. Children color the striped squares in the same order each time, ending up with three of each color spread across the board.

9. Participants color any two hearts with each of the four colors. Then they choose one of their colors for shading the *Back* spaces and a different color for shading the *Forward* spaces.

10. Retreatants place their paper fastener (brad) in the center of their straw and attach it to the center of the spinner, pressing it through the folder and opening it flat against the back.

11. Optional: Retreat helpers can laminate the game boards or place clear contact paper over them.

How to Play the Game—*(Use sample to demonstrate if others are being laminated)* For 2, 3, or 4 players.

Players line up their buttons along the shapes at the start end of the board. Diamond spins first. (S)he moves her button to the first game board square available that matches the color where the spinner has landed. *When landing on a heart with initials, players read them aloud.* Circle spins next and moves her button to the first game board square that matches her spinner point in color. Triangle spins third and square fourth, repeating the same pattern as diamond and circle. On every turn, a player spins and moves to the next color-matched game board square. The game is over (quick version) in twenty minutes or (longer version) when the first player reaches finish in the exact number of moves. Either way, the score is kept by noting the number of times the words "I'm sorry" and "You're forgiven" are used in that time period. All players "win" when participants exchange forgiveness.

Announce to the children: It's almost time to move to your next prayer activity. Please help me get ready for the next group by setting up the table the way it was when you arrived. *(To the final group, give directions about how to put the supplies away.)*

Activity 2: Story as Prayer
Story: *Lilly's Purple Plastic Purse* by Kevin Henkes (New York: Greenwillow Books, 1996)

As the children listen to and discuss the literature, talk about the focus of the retreat (p. 34).

Greet the children.
(As retreatants enter the room, designate a space where they can put their belongings, then invite them to sit where they can see the pictures of the book.)

Raise your hand if you've heard this story before. Wonderful. If you have, let's not tell the others what happens so they can enjoy their experience, too.

This is a time of prayer. Let's get ready to listen to what God wants us to hear in this story. Are you in a comfortable position? Let's all take a deep breath and let it out a little at a time.

Introduce the story.
Our book is called *Lilly's Purple Plastic Purse,* written and illustrated by Kevin Henkes.

This is the story of a girl who brought a special treasure to show her friends. One of the characters in this story may remind you of Jesus by the way he or she acts. Be watching for that part. We'll talk about it together after we finish the book.

Read the story, taking ample time to show the pictures.

(Using voice intonations, pauses, and a prayerful assurance that God is speaking to the children through the reading of this story, read the book aloud. Allow time for the children to be touched by the words as well as the illustrations. At the conclusion, close the book gently and allow a moment of "think time.")

Talk about the story.

▲ First I'd like to hear from someone who imagined a different main character in this same situation. Did any of you try that? *(Listen to responses and ask what that person might have brought to share. If there are none, proceed.)*

▲ In Lilly's case, what were her prized possessions? *(Movie star sunglasses with glittery diamonds and a new purple plastic purse.)*

▲ How did Lilly react when her teacher took them away? *(She drew an unflattering picture of him and put it where he'd find it.)*

▲ Have you ever felt like Lilly did at that moment? She really wanted to get even with Mr. Slinger for the hurt she felt.

▲ What did the teacher do at the end of the day? *(He complimented her on her belongings and reminded her not to disturb the class with them.)*

▲ And there was more. What did Lilly find in her purse?" *(A note and tasty snacks.)*

▲ How did Lilly feel then? *(Simply awful.)*

▲ What did she do next? *(She apologized in writing and brought him a homemade gift of tasty snacks.)*

▲ Let's look at the page where Lilly goes to school the next day. *(Hold up the "really, really, really sorry" page.)* Lilly and Mr. Slinger practice something that we're doing on our retreat—Reconciliation! My favorite part is when Mr. Slinger asks Lilly what they should do about the note. Does he yell at her? Does he call her names? *(No.)*

▲ Have you been thinking about the character that reminds you of Jesus? Which one was it? *(Encourage children to explain why this character was like Jesus. Affirm all responses.)* Did that person bring someone back into a loving relationship where they felt more peaceful and better about themselves?"

▲ Knowing God forgives us endlessly, we learn to forgive others in the same way. Who in the story received forgiveness? *(Lilly.)*

▲ What did Lilly learn about reconciliation? *(We can both give and receive forgiveness. Affirm all answers.)*

(Hold up the book with the cover facing the children.) When you're telling your family about the book you read during the retreat today, remember this title. Let's say it together: *Lilly's Purple Plastic Purse.*

Alternate Story

If the first choice of literature for this session is unavailable, substitute *The Conversation Club* by Diane Stanley (New York: Macmillan Publishing Company, 1990).

Introduction:

Peter Fieldmouse, the new kid on the block, felt completely overwhelmed by his new friends' club. Before the arrival of Peter on the scene, these characters were all seemingly happy meeting on Thursdays to talk. Each was an expert in a field. The problem was that no one was a listening expert until the arrival of Peter. Peter Fieldmouse helped his new neighbors see the error of their ways. This loving Jesus figure taught them a peaceful solution to conflict.

Reading:

(For the purpose of this retreat and to stay within time constraints, delete the first chapter of the book. The characters Peter, Charlie, Nancy, Fay, Pearl, and Sam are all reintroduced in chapter two.)

Discussion:

▲ Sam asked Peter, "Are we doing it right?" Sam really *wanted* reconciliation, even though he found it difficult at first. What does that say to you about living a life of reconciliation? *(Like many things in life, the more we do something, the better we get at it.)*

▲ *(Refer to last page.)* Why was it the best story they had ever heard? *(They really listened.)*

▲ Prayer is talking *and* listening to God. Is Peter's advice to the animals something that can help us when we pray? How? *(It takes practice listening to God in prayer to hear what God might want to say to us.)*

▲ At one point in the story Peter says that his house is nicer with friends in it. Through this next week, notice what's nicer about your own house when you practice reconciliation.

Activity 3: The Heart Room Prayer

Weave the focus of the retreat throughout the children's experience of The Heart Room Prayer.

(Greet the children as they arrive, then invite them to sit in a circle with you. Be sure the circle is large enough that there is room between the children and they don't touch each other. Welcome the children.)

(Ask the children to name someone they think is very important in our world today. These can be sports figures, actors or actresses, members of rock groups, or a

person they consider a hero/heroine. Using seven of the cards, print the suggested names. Ask the group to name someone in our society who does not receive respect, or someone who is friendless. Print those names on the remaining card. Set aside.)

I'd like to show you a way you can pray and talk with Jesus. It's important to know, though, that Jesus isn't somewhere far away. Jesus lives within each one of us, in a place deep inside. I call this place the heart room. Your heart room is a place where it's quiet, where you can go anytime you want to and place yourself in the presence of Jesus, your friend.

It helps me to close my eyes and tune out any sounds. Let's all close our eyes. Don't worry that you'll be the only one. I'll keep my own eyes open to make sure it's safe for everyone. All of us have our eyes closed so we won't be distracted.

I'll lead you now through some helps for praying in our heart room. First, take a deep breath to help you relax. Fine. Let's take another deep breath. We all have our eyes closed. As I lead you through this type of prayer please use my suggestions to make pictures in your mind.

Now I'd like to read a parable, or story, that Jesus told his followers. As you listen to the story, decide what you think was Jesus' reason for telling this particular parable to his friends.

We want to actually be *in* the story, so I want to invite you to travel through a time machine and go back with me almost 2,000 years ago. It's around the year 33, and Jesus is a young man. We have no cars now that we live in Jesus' time. We have no television sets, and telephones have not yet been invented. We've been walking with Jesus along the edge of a large lake called Tiberias. Can you hear the water in the background? *(Pause.)* Some people who've been fishing, and some who've been working in the fields, come and join us.

A couple of shepherds come with their sheep. They stay behind the people, though, so the sheep don't wander off. People of all ages are here. Imagine what the people look like. *(Pause.)* Some of the little kids run up to Jesus to sit down near him. What does Jesus look like? Try to get a picture of him in your mind. *(Pause.)* What color is his hair? Is it curly? Straight? Long? Short? *(Pause.)* Now look at his face. Is he smiling? How does he look at you? *(Pause.)* When you look at his face do you feel peaceful, happy? What are your feelings when you look at Jesus' face? How is Jesus dressed? What color is his skin? *(Pause.)*

Pick a place where you would like to sit. Are you there with your family, or your friends, or are you there alone? The crowd gets quiet and Jesus begins to speak out loud so everyone can hear him. Settle in and listen to what Jesus is saying. *(Slowly read Matthew 18:10-14.)*

[Jesus said:] "Don't be cruel to any of these little ones! I promise you that their angels are always with my Father in heaven. Let me ask you this. What would you do if you had a hundred sheep and one of them wandered off? Wouldn't you leave the ninety-nine on the hillside and go look for the one that had wandered away? I am sure that finding it would make you happier than having the ninety-nine that never wandered off. That's how it is with your Father in heaven. He doesn't want any of these little ones to be lost."

We've just heard Jesus speak. He told us how important each one of us is to God. We're so important, in fact, that if we wander away from God by doing something bad, God will come looking for us even though God has many, many people to care about. When we stop being close to God, this is what we call sin. But God wants us to come back and be friends again, so God forgives us right away. This is Reconciliation. God never wants any of us to feel the sadness of being away from God.

Picture yourself, now, getting up and moving closer to Jesus to talk to him about what you just heard. *(Pause.)* Make yourself comfortable next to Jesus. He's there only for you. Talk to Jesus about a time you felt like you had done something wrong. What would you like to say to Jesus? In our heart room, we don't have to worry that we might say the wrong thing or that Jesus might not understand us. We can tell Jesus anything. I'll stop for a short time and you can tell Jesus about a time you felt you had wandered away from God by doing something bad. Tell him what it felt like. Jesus might also want to say something to you. So listen... *(Wait 90 seconds.)*

It's time to go now. Say goodbye to Jesus in whatever way you'd like. Wave, hug him, or say some simple words. *(Pause.)* Tell Jesus you'll come back to your heart room again. *(Pause.)* Now imagine yourself walking back to our room here. *(Pause.)*

When you're ready, please open your eyes.

Sometimes it helps to look back on what happened during prayer in our heart rooms. What were some of the things you pictured in this story? Was there anything that surprised you about what you saw and heard? How did you feel when you were in your heart room? Did you have an easy time talking to Jesus? Do you believe he heard you? Did Jesus say something to you? Sometimes we hear

Jesus and sometimes we don't. That's natural. *(Allow children time to share.)*

(Pass out seven of the cards that name the important people the class suggested earlier. Have each child hold a card so the others can read them.)

Look at the names of the people on these cards. Why are they important? *(Allow time for children to respond.)*

(Now hold up the card with the "non-important" names on it.) What makes these people different from the important people? Would you say the names on this card are the little people or the big people in the eyes of our world?

Listen once again to the parable. When you hear the part about big, important people, hold up the cards with their names on it. When you hear about little people, hold up that card. *(Reread Matthew 18:10-14.)*

I noticed that no one held up the important names. And I noticed that the one card with the less important names was the card you held up. Hmmmmm... It seems that these are the "little ones" Jesus is talking about in his parable.

Have you ever felt like one of the less important people, or one of the "little ones?" Sometimes, when we feel bad about something we've done wrong, we feel less important or not good enough, like the "little ones" Jesus talked about. Think to yourself of a time when you felt this way, perhaps the time you told Jesus about a few minutes ago in prayer. *(Pause.)* Remember that because God made us, we are good. God loves us so much, God never wants us to know the sadness of feeling unimportant or forgotten. God will always bring us back.

Now that you've had a chance to talk to Jesus in your heart room, you can do this anytime you want. There's no place off-limits for talking to Jesus, no time that's too early or too late. You can repeat this prayer anytime you'd like to talk to Jesus. The heart room has been a good, peaceful place, hasn't it?

Remember what we did here in our retreat. I hope you have many happy and prayerful times with Jesus in your heart room whenever you pray this way again.

Snack
cookies and milk

Adult-Child Sharing Time
After the adult session, parents or adult retreat leaders join their children in the snack room to begin their sharing time. If weather permits, retreatants can go outside for a nature walk. If not, they might want to find a corner to sit in, take

a walk through the church, spread out blankets throughout the room, or even create forts out of blankets to sit in for privacy. We allow twenty minutes for adult-child sharing time, asking all participants to return to the gathering room at the allotted time for our closing.

The questions on p. 214 can facilitate adult-child sharing.

If time remains, parents or adult leaders can help children compose a song to a familiar tune, using the focus of the retreat.

For example:
(To the tune of "My Darlin' Clementine")

> I am sorry, I am sorry,
> I am sorry I say to you.
> I forgive you, I forgive you,
> And I love you, yes I do.

(To accommodate children who are not auditory learners, print the lyrics of each song on a large poster board and display.)

Closing Prayer

The children can close with song, teaching each other the lyrics their group composed. Following the prayer of joyful song, an adult facilitator leads the children in the following litany:

Adult:	I invite all of you to join me in prayer. First, I'll say something to God for all of us. Then you say, "God forgives us, guaranteed."
Adult:	Loving God, you love us so much that no matter how far we wander away from you by doing bad things, you forgive us.
Children:	God forgives us, guaranteed.
Adult:	Loving God, when you forgive us we feel loved by you.
Children:	God forgives us, guaranteed.
Adult:	Loving God, when you forgive us we feel more peaceful and loving.
Children:	God forgives us, guaranteed.
Adult:	Loving God, because you forgive us so freely, we try to forgive those who hurt us, too.
Children:	God forgives us, guaranteed.
Adult:	Loving God, you forgive us in the sacrament of Reconciliation.
Children:	God forgives us, guaranteed.

Invite children to join hands and say the Our Father.

3-Good Friends Retreat

(Matthew 4:18-22)

If giving a family retreat that includes three- to six-year-olds, coordinate with the retreat entitled "Fish" from *Parent-Child Retreats: Spiritual Experiences for Children Ages 3-6 and Their Parents* (Living the Good News, 1997).

Focus

The foundation of this retreat is the connectedness of all people because of the indwelling of the Spirit of Jesus. The ramifications of this spiritual truth are far-reaching. Because God dwells within, God is with us in all of life. God is the presence we bring to each other. And inherent in the interplay of the elements of the Great Commandment to love God, and to love others as we love ourselves, is that in loving each other, we love God. We attempt to heighten children's awareness of this dynamic in their friendships.

We honor the idea that children are forming their image of a loving God. The names we call God during retreat can help create a positive image of the God who is Love. As children are exposed to more of the scriptures, they'll hear different names for God and Jesus. We help them understand the significance of these names, yet always emphasize that God is love. It is love—God—that bonds us to each other and makes our presence a spiritual one.

We introduce the fish-shaped *ichthys*, which is the Christian symbol for the unity of those who follow Jesus. In the early Church, Christians used this symbol to connect with each other without fear of persecution. *Ichthys* means "fish" in Greek and comes from the first letters of the Greek words for "Jesus Christ, Son of God, Savior." As good friends with each other and with Jesus, our retreatants are bonded in the Son of God.

> The focus of the retreat can be summarized in three statements:
> ▲ Through everything that happens in our life, good or bad, Jesus is there.
> ▲ We are a presence of God's love to the people in our lives.
> ▲ By being good friends with others, we become better friends with Jesus.

To help make these truths relevant to children, we appeal to their computer expertise. We ask the retreatants to apply problem-solving skills to unscramble two magazine articles of supposedly disparate genres: religious and adventure. What the children discover is how difficult it is to separate the two. In fact, their integration is quite natural. This provides a paradigm for the spiritual life: God's Spirit has joined our spirits[1] and as this indwelling transforms us, we discover how difficult it is to separate the everyday from the spiritual. Their connection is natural, and these young retreatants are learning to open their eyes to this truth.

Preparations Before the Retreat

1. Meet as a team to pray, read, discuss, understand, and interiorize the focus and scriptural basis for the retreat.
2. Discern which team members will be responsible for the gathering presentation, each of the three children's activities, and the adult retreat section, if there is one.
3. If this is to be a family retreat, choose an adult retreat topic from the section entitled Outlines for Parent Sessions (pp. 163-184). If parents will not be present, prepare a letter to send home for parent-child follow-up enrichment (p. 188).

4. Divide the following preparation responsibilities. Use the gifts of the community to lighten the load. Parents, teenagers, school children, and senior citizens can all help prepare.

Make nametags in three colors.

Collect materials for the environment.
Bible
picture of Jesus
sample souvenir
book for story
bulletin board or poster bearing the ichthys symbol *(Following the retreat, children can surround the ichthys with one of the paper fish they created during the Story as Prayer session. For added decoration, cover the poster or bulletin board with blue plastic wrap.)*

Prepare the retreat souvenir (p. 52).
First, gather materials for each retreatant:
▲ five recloseable plastic bags, any size
▲ two pieces cardstock *(as long and as wide as the distance from the bottom of the bag to 3/4 inch below the zipper)*
▲ blackline masters (see Appendix, p 202-203.)

For retreatants to share:
▲ markers/crayons
▲ scissors

Second, do the advance preparation:
1. Stitch the plastic bags together by hand or machine into a five-page book, or staple the bags together, then cover the stapled area with masking tape as binding for safety.
2. Make a sample book to show during the retreat.
2. Copy one of each blackline master for each retreatant.

Locate the story.
Obtain *In God's Name* by Sandy Eisenberg Sasso (Woodstock, Vermont: Jewish Lights Publishing, 1994). Gather materials: 3 notepad size ichthys-shaped papers for each retreatant, and pencils, pens, or markers for writing on the fish. If unable to locate the first literature choice, substitute *Roxaboxen* by Alice McLerran (Penguin Books: New York, 1991) and change the letter to parents.

Prepare for the gathering presentation.

Duplicate the mixed-up story (p. 200-201) onto an overhead transparency, copy it onto butcher paper, or write each sentence on a poster strip backed with sticky magnetic strips. Make two large cue cards with the words "Stay calm" on one and "Think hard" on the other.

Become familiar with the heart room prayer (p. 56).

Gather materials: a large ball of string or yarn, and newsprint and marker or a blackboard and chalk.

Purchase groceries and prepare the snack.

fish-shaped crackers and beverages

Duplicate the Adult-Child Sharing Form (p. 214) or letter to parents (p. 188).

Preparations the Day of the Retreat

1. Gather as a team and pray.
2. Set out nametags and safety pins or tape *(warning: no straight pins or strings)*. Have exactly as many nametags as retreatants, and equal numbers of nametags for each color group.
3. Have each retreat team member wear a different colored nametag. This will later help the children divide into groups for their activities.
4. On top of a piano or table, create the environment in the gathering room with an arrangement that reflects the theme of the retreat. Include the book that will be read during the retreat, a sample of the souvenir the children will make, and a Bible.
5. Gather all the materials for the retreat souvenir and set out on tables in the room that will be used for this activity.
6. Spread out so that at least one team member is greeting the retreatants as they arrive, another is bringing retreatants (and parents) to the gathering room, a third is waiting in the gathering room, and a fourth is directing parents and younger siblings to the nursery.
7. Begin the retreat by warmly greeting the retreatants, then introducing the team members.

Gathering Presentation

Attention, everybody, we have an emergency. Now don't panic. There's no problem so great we can't solve it if we stay calm and do our best reasoning. I repeat: Stay calm.

Now, take in a deep breath. *(Inhale loudly and dramatically.)* Let's all say this together: Stay calm. *(Motion the children to repeat.)* Think hard. *(Children repeat.)* Good. May I have two volunteers to help me? *(Choose a girl and a boy. Instruct each one to hold up a cue card so that the others will say the phrase that's on their card.)* Let's have this group say, "Stay calm" and this group say, "Think hard." We desperately need each other if we're going to get a grip on the problem. Ready? *(Lead the two groups in 3 or 4 rounds, alternating "Stay calm" and "Think hard.")*

Here's the problem: A famous national religious magazine and a famous children's adventure magazine found that their files had accidentally been mixed up. The result of this rare and bizarre, who-would-ever-believe-something-like-this-could-happen scrambling of files is that only one article, rather than two, appeared. It's up to us to fix the problem and create two separate articles, one for the religious magazine, and one for the adventure magazine. The problem is that some lines showed up only once, but were meant for both stories. Other lines were meant to be used in either one or the other. Does that sound confusing?

Remember, stay calm.... Think hard.... That's the idea. Let's get to work. I'm going to put the article up here so we can all read it. *(Place the transparency of the article on the overhead projector or display the article written on butcher paper. See pp. 200-201.)*

Friendship is Life-Giving

JESUS' LIFE-GIVING FRIENDSHIP IS FRIEND HELPS BEST FRIEND

David and Marissa were best friends. Jesus is our best friend. One day they were hiking when suddenly David lost his footing and tumbled down the cliff. Sometimes, when we feel scared, darkness grabs us like a kidnapper with a gunny sack. His fear gripped at him like a surgeon holding a throbbing appendix. But in everything that happens in our life, good and bad, our special friend Jesus is there. Marissa reached out and saved him. His friendship is life-giving. David realized he had the best friend a person could ever want.

Children's Activities

The following three children's activities run simultaneously, and the children rotate through them until they've been to all three.

Activity 1: Art as Prayer—Retreat Souvenir

The retreatants will make Jesus Zipper Bag Books. The book is a special place where children can keep mementos from today's retreat as well as items from home that are important to them, and about which they can to talk to Jesus. As the children create their souvenir, talk about the focus of the retreat (p. 49).

Gather participants around the materials table, where each will find a preassembled five-page plastic zipper-bag book and blackline masters.

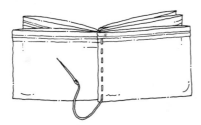 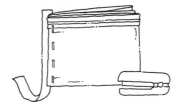

1. Children place a cover page in the first plastic bag (page 1) and in the last bag (page 5).
2. Children label the cover *Prayer,* write their names on it and illustrate it. Children cut out blackline masters. Explain: Besides this session where we're using art to praise God, those are the other two retreat sessions today. *(Note— Children who come to this session first will have been to neither of the other two sessions. Those who arrive second will have completed either Prayer or Story as Prayer first. The final group will have been both places and can complete this task now. The leader will briefly describe the other two sessions so that all participants can draw pictures for their book at this time.)*
3. (See appendix pp. 202-203.) On page 2 of the book, children write the title of today's story: *In God's Name* by Sandy Eisenberg Sasso. On p. 3, they draw something to help recall the story. *(Note: Either display the book, describe the characters and setting, or give a brief summary so the children who have not yet been to the story session can make a quick sketch.)*
4. On page 4 of the book, retreatants draw something to remind themselves that they can talk to Jesus in their heart, any time. *(Note: To help those who have not yet been to their heart room, instruct the children to draw a picture of themselves talking to Jesus in a favorite place.)*

5. Children who finish early can illustrate the back cover.

Announce to the children: Use this special memento you've made today to share your experiences of Jesus with an adult at home. It's almost time to move to your next prayer session. Please help me get ready for the next group by setting up the table the way it was when you arrived. *(To the final group, give directions about how to put supplies away.)*

Activity 2: Story as Prayer

Story: *In God's Name* by Sandy Eisenberg Sasso (Woodstock, Vermont: Jewish Lights Publishing, 1994)

As the children listen to and discuss the literature, talk about the focus of the retreat (p. 49).

Greet the children.

(As retreatants enter the room, designate a space where they can put their belongings, then invite the children to sit where they can see the pictures in the book.)

Raise your hand if you've heard this story before. Wonderful. If you have, let's not tell the others what happens so they can enjoy their experience, too.

This is a time of prayer. Let's get ready to listen to what God wants us to hear in this story. Are you in a comfortable position? Let's all take a deep breath and let it out a little at a time.

Introduce the story.

This fable is about the many ways people understand God. This book celebrates people's belief in one God, even when they don't all believe just exactly alike. Be ready to hear about the Spirit of God alive in people. Listen carefully to the end of the story. The book is called *In God's Name*. The author is Sandy Eisenberg Sasso.

Read the story, taking ample time to show the pictures.

(Using voice intonations, pauses, and a prayerful sense of awe, read the book aloud. Allow time for children to be touched by the words as well as the illustrations. At the conclusion, close the book gently and allow a moment of "think time.")

Talk about the story.

▲ Let's read that last part together again: "*Everyone listened. Most of all, God.*" After reading that, does it explain what we said at the beginning of this retreat: "In everything that happens in our lives, good or bad, Jesus is there"?

▲ The author wrote, "They knelt by a lake that was clear and quiet like a mirror, God's mirror." How was the lake like God's mirror? *(We mirror God's love to the people in our lives.)*

▲ What are some of your favorite names for God in this story?

54

▲ What were some of the names Jesus' friends, the apostles, called him? *(Friend, Brother, Lord, Master, Teacher, Messiah, Good Shepherd, Light of the World, Prince of Peace)*

▲ This story talked about the Spirit of God being alive in people. How might that explain what we said earlier in the retreat, that by being good friends with others, we become better friends with Jesus?

(Hold up the book with the cover facing the children.) When you're telling your family about the book you read during the retreat today, remember this title. Let's say it together: *In God's Name.* The author is Sandy Eisenberg Sasso.

(Distribute three ichthys shapes and writing tools to each retreatant.) This fish shape has a special name: ichthys. It's the symbol Christians use to let each other know that they love Jesus. A long time ago, people who loved Jesus were punished. The way these people communicated with each other without being caught was to draw an ichthys. Ichthys is a Greek word, and the first letters of the word stand for "Jesus Christ, Son of God, Savior."

Take a minute to think about your favorite names for Jesus. Write one name for Jesus on each fish shape. Friends often have a pet name or nickname for each other like buddy, pal, girlfriend. Use your special name for Jesus tonight before you fall asleep. Place the fish in a section of your zipper bag book now. *(They may not have it with them if they haven't been to the art session yet. That group should keep it with them until they have a book to put it into.)*

Announce to the children: It's time to move on to the next session. Check to be sure lids are on writing tools and there is no paper on the floor.

Alternate Story

If the first choice of literature for this retreat session is unavailable, use *Roxaboxen* by Alice McLerran (Penguin Books: New York, 1991).

Introduction:

Marian (the author's mother), her sisters, and friends, created an imaginary town on a hillside covered with rocks and wooden boxes and named it Roxaboxen. In the minds and hearts of the children who played there, that magical world laid the foundations for later relationships. It's about how beautifully children can create because of their wonderful imaginations.

As we read this story together, we know that in everything that happens, Jesus is there. So, let's go with Marian, her three sisters, Charles who is twelve, Eleanor, Jamie, and Paul to a place where some days were spent creating their town and "other days you might just find a treasure without even looking." In this imaginary town, Marian was the mayor, streets and houses were made of white stones, and round black pebbles became the money. The children played for hours in Roxaboxen where there was no television, no videos, only the ideas they brought to life with their imaginative playtime.

Reading:
(While reading, point out that the children were a presence of God's love to one another. Help children notice that like our friend Jesus, "Roxaboxen was always waiting, always there" for the children. It was a safe place, a place full of happy, peaceful memories. Being with Jesus gives us similar feelings. And we can go to Jesus anytime we want.)

Discussion:
▲ What was so special about Roxaboxen? *(The children had built it themselves and created their own sense of community there.)*
▲ By being good friends with others we learn to become better friends with Jesus. Name someone who is your friend who helps you be better friends with Jesus.
▲ When you grow up, what will you tell your own children about Jesus?
▲ Who in this story reminded you of Jesus?

Activity 3: The Heart Room Prayer

Weave the focus of the retreat throughout the children's experience of the heart room prayer.

(Greet the children as they arrive, then invite them to sit in a circle with you. Be sure the circle is large enough that there is room between the children and they don't touch each other. Welcome the children.)

If you were going on a fishing trip with your friends, what would be some important things to bring? *(As the children volunteer suggestions, write the items on a blackboard or large sheet of newsprint.)* Now let's change the scene a little. You find out there isn't much room in the car or truck, and you have to leave some of the things behind. What would you scratch off our list? *(Guide the children to eliminate everything except the bare necessities.)* Look at the list now. Do you think we would have what we need to go fishing? Let's leave that list for now and think about something else. Let's all stand in a circle.

I'm going to hold onto the end of this ball of yarn/string. I'll throw the ball I'm holding to someone in the circle. Here, Andrew. Catch. Now say your name, then hold onto the yarn and throw the ball of yarn to someone else in the circle. Go ahead and try it. Good. You threw it to Molly. Now say your name and throw the ball of yarn to someone else. Remember to hold onto the yarn when you throw the ball. *(Throwing the yarn will make a web-like pattern as it criss-crosses the group. Make certain each participant holds onto the yarn before throwing the ball to the next person.)*

What do you notice the yarn has done to our circle? That's right. It has connected us. Right now the yarn is the reason we're connected to each other, but there's a person who connects us in even more important ways—our friend Jesus. Think about this: Jesus is connected to us and we're connected to Jesus. In fact, we are all connected to each other in many ways. *(Ask a volunteer to go to each person and rewind the yarn into a ball.)* Let's all sit down again and talk about how we are all connected in Jesus.

Jesus is present in our lives, no matter what is going on. Everything about us is important to Jesus. Remember our list of fishing items? It wasn't too hard to cross off some things that weren't absolutely necessary, was it? But if Jesus were making a list about what was important about each of us, he wouldn't be able to cross anything off. Jesus is interested in all that goes on in our lives.

I'm going to divide you into pairs right now. *(Ask the children to count off 1-2, 1-2, 1-2 until all have been assigned a number. Instruct all the 1s to turn and face a 2. Children will do an activity in these pairs.)* With your partner, think of one good thing that could happen in your life and one bad thing. *(Allow time for pairs to discuss.)*

Let's hear some of the things you and your partner came up with. What is one good thing and one bad thing that could happen in your life? *(List on newsprint or blackboard.)* Look at this list. Is there anything Jesus would not be interested in? That's right, not a single one. Jesus is with us in every one of these events, good and bad. What does that tell you about God's love?

I'd like to read you a short story from Matthew's gospel. It's about a group of people and their faith that Jesus would be with them no matter what. As you and I discovered in making our list, there isn't any reason why God would not be with us always. As I read, see if you can discover what these people did when they knew Jesus would be with them.

(Read Matthew 4:18-22.)

"While Jesus was walking along the shore of Lake Galilee, he saw two brothers. One was Simon, also known as Peter, and the other was Andrew. They were fisher-

men, and they were casting their net into the lake. Jesus said to them, 'Come with me! I will teach you how to bring in people instead of fish.' Right then the two brothers dropped their nets and went with him. Jesus walked on until he saw James and John, the sons of Zebedee. They were in a boat with their father, mending their nets. Jesus asked them to come with him too. Right away they left the boat and their father and went with Jesus."

What did you notice about the people's reaction to Jesus when he invited them to be with him? Do you think their reaction was reasonable, to leave everything they had and follow Jesus? What was the promise Jesus made to them? Does that sound funny, to "bring in people"? Do you think Jesus really meant they were going to catch people in a fishing net? What could he have meant? Jesus wanted friends to help him teach all people that God is with us always. It was a simple message, but it would take a lot of people to spread the word. By "bringing in people" they could be a presence of God's love to the people they met.

We, too, can be a presence of God's love to the people we meet. And what's interesting is that by being good friends with others, we become better friends with Jesus. Remember how Jesus connects all of us, just as the yarn connected us? Being connected by Jesus means that the more we love each other, the more we love Jesus. In fact, after Jesus died, all the people who loved Jesus tried to stay connected to one another. They let each other know they were followers of Jesus by drawing a fish shape, called an ichthys, in the sand. That's how important it is to be a presence of God to each other.

I'd like to show you a way you can pray and talk with Jesus. It's important to know, though, that Jesus isn't somewhere far away. Jesus lives within each one of us, in a place deep inside. I call this place the heart room. Your heart room is a place where it's quiet, where you can go anytime you want to and place yourself in the presence of Jesus, your friend.

It helps me to close my eyes and tune out any sounds. Let's all close our eyes. Don't worry that you'll be the only one. I'll keep my own eyes open to make sure it's safe for everyone. All of us have our eyes closed so we won't be distracted.

I'll lead you now through some helps for praying in our heart room. First, take a deep breath to help you relax. Fine. Let's take another deep breath. We all have our eyes closed. As I lead you through this type of prayer please use my suggestions to make pictures in your mind.

58

We're all in a fishing boat in the middle of the sea. *(Pause.)* Listen to the sounds of the waves. Smell the air. *(Pause.)* Watch the other people who are fishing. *(Pause.)* Someone is with us on the boat, which is our heart room. It's Jesus. *(Pause.)* What does he look like? What color is his hair? Is it curly? Straight? Long? Short? *(Pause.)* Now look at his face. Is he smiling? How does he look at you? *(Pause.)* When you look at his face do you feel peaceful, happy? What are your feelings when you look at Jesus' face? How is Jesus dressed? What color is his skin?

Jesus sits down next to you. *(Pause.)* Make yourself comfortable next to Jesus. He's there only for you. What would you like to say to Jesus? In our heart room, we don't have to worry that we might say the wrong thing or that Jesus might not understand us. Knowing we're with such an incredibly good friend, let's take a minute to talk with Jesus right now. I'll stop for a short time and you can tell Jesus whatever you would like. Jesus might also want to say something to you. So listen... *(Wait 60 seconds.)*

It's time to go now. Say goodbye to Jesus in whatever way you'd like. Wave, hug him, or say some simple words. *(Pause.)* Tell Jesus you'll come back to your heart room again. *(Pause.)* Now imagine yourself coming back to our room here. *(Wait 30 seconds.)*

When you're ready, please open your eyes.

Sometimes it helps to look back on what happened in prayer in our heart rooms. How did you feel when you were in your heart room? Did you have an easy time talking to Jesus? Do you believe he heard you? Did Jesus say anything to you? Sometimes we hear Jesus and sometimes we don't. That's natural. *(Allow children time to share.)*

Now that you've had a chance to talk to Jesus in your heart room, you can do this anytime you want. There's no place off-limits for talking to Jesus, no time that's too early or too late. You can repeat this prayer anytime you'd like to talk to Jesus. It's been a good, peaceful place, hasn't it?

Remember what we did here in our retreat. I hope you have many happy and prayerful times with Jesus in your heart room when you pray this way again.

Snack
fish crackers and beverage

Adult-Child Sharing Time

After the adult session, parents or adult retreat leaders join their children in the snack room to begin their sharing time. If weather permits, retreatants can go outside for a nature walk. If not, they might want to find a corner to sit in, take a walk through the church, spread out blankets throughout the room, or even create forts out of blankets to sit in for privacy. We allow approximately twenty minutes for adult-child sharing time, asking all participants to return to the gathering room at the allotted time for our closing.

The questions on p. 214 can facilitate adult-child sharing.

If time remains, parents or adult leaders can help children compose a song to a familiar tune, using the focus of the retreat.

For example:
(To the tune "Hi-Ho" from "Snow White")

> Good friends, good friends,
> Since Jesus is our friend,
> When we love and care,
> When we trust and share,
> We're friends, good friends.

(To accommodate children who are not auditory learners, print the lyrics of each song on a large poster board and display.)

Closing Prayer

The children can close with song, teaching each other the lyrics their group composed. Following the prayer of joyful song, an adult facilitator leads the children in the following litany:

Adult:	I invite all of you to join me in prayer. First, I'll say something to Jesus for all of us. Then you say, "You are our friend."
Adult:	Jesus who loves us, through all that happens in our life, you are there.
Children:	You are our friend.
Adult:	Jesus who loves us, in the good and bad, you are there with us.
Children:	You are our friend.
Adult:	Jesus who loves us, we are a presence of your love to the people in our lives.
Children:	You are our friend.
Adult:	Jesus who loves us, by being better friends with you, we become better friends with others.
Children:	You are our friend.
Adult:	Jesus who loves us, help us to love other people as you have loved us.
Children:	You are our friend.

Invite children to join hands and say the Our Father.

Note
1. Richard Hauser, *In His Spirit* (Ramsey, N.J.: Paulist Press, 1982), 8.

4-Good News Retreat

(Luke 10:21; Matthew 19:13; Matthew 18:1-5; 1 John 4:10, 19)

If giving a family retreat that includes three- to six-year-olds, coordinate with the retreat entitled "Bubbles" from *Parent-Child Retreats: Spiritual Experiences for Children Ages 3-6 and Their Parents* (Living the Good News, 1997).

Focus

The flaws in human love have saddened us all. Many have had the experience of trying to initiate friendship, then being rejected. But John tells us that God loved us *first* (1 Jn. 4:10, 19). For some, this can lift quite a burden: the fear of rejection, the task of always being the initiator, the yearning to know we're lovable. The Good News is that God has invited *us* into a love relationship; all we have to do is say "yes."

Our life abounds with God's love. For some, it's obvious. For others, it's not so clear. But for all of us, God's love becomes apparent as we grow in awareness of the ways God loves us. It's particularly significant how God loves us through other people. We invite children to look for people who are loving and giving, who exude kindness and, therefore, remind them of Jesus. We encourage the children to also examine ways they themselves are like Jesus. For some children, their encounter with the adult retreat leaders may be one of the rare times they've witnessed loving kindness. For these children especially, learning to notice how God loves them is essential.

Our dependence on God helps us develop the stance of noticing God's presence. The nature of childhood necessarily places children in a position of dependence, and we want to ensure that their dependence develops into healthy trust. The more children experience times of trust in their human relationships, the easier it is to extend that trust to God.

> The focus of the retreat can be summarized in four statements:
> ▲ We use the expression "Good News" when we talk about all that God's love means to us.
> ▲ An important aspect of God's love is that God loved us first (1 Jn. 4:10, 19).
> ▲ One way God shows love to us is through people we meet.
> ▲ It takes practice recognizing when and how God is making God's love known to us.

Preparations Before the Retreat

1. Meet as a team to pray, read, discuss, understand, and interiorize the focus and scriptural basis for the retreat.
2. Discern which team members will be responsible for the gathering presentation, each of the three children's activities, and the adult retreat section, if there is one.
3. If this is to be a family retreat, choose an adult retreat topic from the section entitled Outlines for Parent Sessions (pp. 163-184). If parents will not be present, prepare materials to send home for parent-child follow-up enrichment (p. 189).
4. Divide preparation responsibilities. Use the gifts of the community to lighten the load. Parents, teenagers, school children, and senior citizens can all help prepare.

Make nametags in three colors.

Collect materials for the environment.

Bible

picture of Jesus

sample souvenir

book for story

three translucent balloons

bulletin board or poster bearing pictures of children of all races and the words
  "We find God in people."

Prepare the retreat souvenir (p. 68).

First, gather materials for each retreatant:

▲ clean empty soda can

▲ aluminum foil, 6 inches square

▲ rubberband

▲ pipe cleaner

▲ blackline master of label sample

▲ enough clear contact paper to cover the can

For retreatants to share:

▲ several plastic buckets, cups, and funnels

▲ water

▲ Dawn or Joy liquid detergent

▲ glycerin (available at pharmacy)

▲ shower curtain or vinyl tablecloth

▲ paper towels

▲ cellophane tape

Second, do the advance preparation.

1. Prepare ingredients of bubble solution for children to make, one cup per
   child:
   1 cup dishwashing liquid, 2 cups warm water, 3-4 tablespoons glycerin, and 1
   teaspoon sugar. (Or 1/2 cup dishwashing liquid and 5 cups clean cold water.)
2. Make sample souvenir for demonstration. Try three kinds of wands.
3. Cut foil squares and can decoration strips.
4. Cut clear contact paper to cover each can.

Locate the story.

Obtain *Ming Lo Moves the Mountain* by Arnold Lobel (New York: Scholastic,
1982).

If unable to locate the first literature choice, substitute *Knots on a Counting Rope* by Bill Martin Jr. and John Archambault (Bantam Doubleday Dell: New York, 1987) and change the letter to parents.

Prepare for the gathering presentation.

Become familiar with the heart room prayer (p. 71).
Materials: Collect a variety of pictures of young children from ages toddler to kindergarten. If possible, have enough pictures for each participant. Bring a bottle of bubble solution, paper bubbles, and writing tools.

Purchase groceries and prepare the snack.
▲ root beer
▲ ice cream
▲ paper cups
▲ spoons
▲ napkins

Duplicate the Adult-Child Sharing Form (p. 214) or letter to parents (p. 189).

Preparations the Day of the Retreat
1. Gather as a team and pray.
2. Set out nametags and safety pins or tape *(warning: no straight pins or strings)*. Have exactly as many nametags as retreatants, and equal numbers of nametags for each color group.
3. Have each retreat team member wear a different colored nametag. This will later help the children divide into groups for their activities.
4. On top of a piano or table, create the environment in the gathering room with an arrangement that reflects the theme of the retreat. Include the book that will be read during the retreat, a sample of the souvenir the children will make, and a Bible.
5. Gather all the materials for the retreat souvenir and set out on tables in the room that will be used for this activity.
6. Spread out so that at least one team member is greeting the retreatants as they arrive, one is bringing retreatants (and parents) to the gathering room, one is waiting in the gathering room, and one is directing parents and younger siblings to the nursery.
7. Begin the retreat by warmly greeting the retreatants, then introducing the team members.

Gathering Presentation

We can't do anything today until we've learned a cheer. Are you ready for this? Are your voices strong? Say *Yes*. Say it louder. Once again, are our voices stronnnnnng?

I think we're ready to do our cheer. Let's divide ourselves into four groups. *(Take a few seconds to divide the crowd into quadrants. No need for anyone to move.)*

Group one, here's your word: *Good*. Let's hear you say it. Loud now. *(Wait.)*

Group two: *News*. Shout it out. *(Wait.)*

Now let's try it one after the other: *Good*, then *News*. *(Practice a few times so the two words flow.)*

Group 3, your word is *God's*—that's *G-o-d*-apostrophe-*s*—*God's*. Let's hear you say it. *(Wait.)*

And Group 4, you'll say *Love*. Let's hear it. *(Wait.)*

Now let's hear groups 3 and 4 say *God's Love*, one after the other. *(Practice a few times so the two words flow.)*

Are you ready to put it all together? We need you to say your word loudly, and precisely after the group before you has said theirs. Group 1-2-3-4. *Good News— God's Love*. Let's try it. *(Point to the quadrants in order and repeat 5-10 times.)*

Nice job, everyone. I'm sure they heard us way over in the next town! God's love *is* good news.

Followers of Jesus—and that's what we are—use the expression "Good News" when we talk about all that God's love means to us. One important thing about God's love is that God loved us first (1 Jn. 4:10, 19). *(Pause.)* God loved us first. *(Pause.)*

Think about what that means. Have you ever tried to be friends with someone who didn't want to be friends with you? Have you ever asked anyone to play, and they said "no" for no good reason? Have you ever thought someone was your best friend, then found out they said something bad about you?

Our feelings can be hurt when we try to make friends with someone. It can be scary to love someone first.

But what we know from the Bible is that God loved us first. We don't ever have to worry that God won't want to be friends with us. When we ask God to be with us, God will never say no, because God loved us first. And we know that Jesus is the best friend we can have. This is all... *(Point to the word quadrants.)* *Good News—God's Love. Good News—God's Love. (Have the children repeat this several times.)*

And there's more Good News. One way God shows us love is through people we meet. Raise your hand if you know at least one person who's really kind to you. Raise your hand if you know someone who is good. Raise your hand if you know someone who has a beautiful and gentle heart.

Here's a little secret I'd like to share with you. Listen... *(Wait.)* The secret has three parts: 1) God loves us through the people who are kind to us. 2) The goodness in all things is God. 3) The beauty in all things is God.

Let me say that secret again. *(Repeat words above.)*

God has a lot of ways to show us God loves us, don't you think? Think about all the loving people... and all the goodness... and all the beauty we see every day. That really is... *(Point to the word quadrants.)* *Good News—God's Love. Good News—God's Love. (Let the children repeat this several times.)*

It takes practice recognizing when and how God is making God's love known to us. I'm going to make a suggestion. Do all of you pray before going to bed at night? *(Pause for responses.)*

My suggestion is to pray this way before you go to bed each night: Think about all the loving people you talked to or played with that day. Then think about what goodness you noticed that day. Was it good people, was it good things that happened, or was it both? Finally, think about what you saw that day that was beautiful. Maybe it was a beautiful sight, or maybe it was a person with a beautiful and gentle heart. I want to say that again. Let's count on our fingers the three ways we can pray. *(Hold up a finger for each suggestion and invite the children to do the same.)* First, we'll think about all the *loving people* we talked to or played with today. Second, we'll think about what *goodness* we noticed today in either people or in things that happened. Third, we'll think about what we saw today that was *beautiful.*

End your prayer by thanking God for loving you first and for loving you in so many ways. Thank God for... *(Point to the word quadrants.)* *Good News—God's Love. Good News—God's Love. (Have the children repeat this several times.)*

We have some fun activities to do now. Let me show you what we'll be doing. *(Show the children the souvenir and story, and tell them they'll also be talking to Jesus.)*

Now look at the color of your nametag. *(Have the children leave the room with the team leader who has the same colored nametag.)*

Children's Activities

The following three children's activities run simultaneously, and the children rotate through them until they've been to all three.

Activity 1: Art as Prayer—Retreat Souvenir

Participants will make and use Good News Bubble Solution, which they can take home as a prayerful reminder of the Good News of God's love.

As the children make their bubble solution, talk about how the four theme statements of the retreat (p. 63) are good news that bubbles over.

Gather retreatants around a bucket which has been placed on a shower curtain or vinyl tablecloth. Have paper towels ready nearby.

1. The leader reads the bubble solution recipe and invites individuals to add the ingredients. Gently stir together.
2. While leader and one group fill the cans with a funnel and cup, the other children color their labels for the outside of the cans. *(Remind children to write their names on the cans.)*
3. Retreatants give their decorated labels to the helpers, who will cover them with clear contact paper to make the labels waterproof.
4. Children make a wand with a pipe cleaner and tape it onto the can to take home.
5. Each child receives a recipe to take home.

Activity 2: Story as Prayer

Story: *Ming Lo Moves the Mountain* by Arnold Lobel (New York: Scholastic, 1982)

As the children listen to and discuss the literature, talk about the focus of the retreat (p. 63).

Greet the children.
(As retreatants enter the room, designate a space where they can put their belongings, then invite the children to sit where they can see the pictures in the book.)

Raise your hand if you've heard this story before. Wonderful. If you have, let's not tell the others what happens so they can enjoy their experience, too.

This is a time of prayer. Let's get ready to listen to what God wants us to hear in this story. Are you in a comfortable position? Let's all take a deep breath and let it out a little at a time.

Introduce the story.
In this story, Ming Lo and his wife love their house, but because it's located at the foot of a mountain, it rains constantly. They decide they need to move the large mountain in order to be happy, and they seek the advice of a wise man.

What about you? Is there something you really love about your house? *(Listen to several responses.)* Well, in this story, the two main characters loved everything about their house—except that huge mountain that brought them unhappiness. They spent a good deal of time trying to move it. When they consulted a wise man about their problem, he made a series of suggestions for moving the mountain. The final suggestion may seem a bit strange to you. You may even have a much better idea of what should be done, but try to see the story through the eyes of Ming Lo or his wife.

Someone in the story might remind you of Jesus. Listen carefully for a character who is loving and caring. This character tries to help. We'll talk about your ideas after we have heard the entire story together.

Arnold Lobel wrote the words and drew the illustrations for *Ming Lo Moves the Mountain.* As you listen to the story remember that God shows love to us in people we meet.

Read the story, taking ample time to show the pictures.
(Using voice intonations, pauses, and a prayerful sense of awe, read the book aloud. Allow time for children to be touched by the words as well as the illustrations. At the conclusion, close the book gently and allow a moment of "think time.")

Parent-Child Retreats

Talk about the story.

▲ What did you think of that? Is there someone who could show us the dance Ming Lo and his wife did? *(Put left foot in back of right foot and right foot in back of left foot again and again)* Who else who would like to join in? Let's have the mountain be right here. *(Gesture towards its location. Have children stand several feet from walls, with enough space to move backwards. Encourage participation.)*

▲ Why were Ming Lo and his wife unhappy? *(The mountain caused stones to break loose, heavy rains to fall, and dark shadows to cover their home.)*

▲ Which character reminded you of Jesus? In what way? *(The wise man helped them in their unhappiness.)*

▲ Do you think God showed love to Ming Lo and his wife? How? *(Through the caring and wisdom of the wise man, Ming Lo and his wife were able to move away from the shadow of the mountain.)*

▲ Ming Lo and his wife truly believed they had the power to move the mountain. What do you believe about Jesus just as strongly as those two characters believed about their power to move the mountain? *(Honor all replies by repeating or rephrasing them. As retreatants teach each other, this is faith sharing in one of its richest moments.)*

(Hold up the book with the cover facing the children.) When you're telling your family about the book you read during the retreat today, remember this title. Let's say it together: *Ming Lo Moves the Mountain*

Announce to the children: Now it's time to move to the next retreat session. Be sure to take any of your belongings with you on your way out. Let's walk together.

Alternate Story

If the first literature choice for this session is unavailable, substitute *Knots on a Counting Rope* by Bill Martin Jr. and John Archambault (New York: Bantam Doubleday Dell, 1987).

(Provide a length of rope or macrame cord that can be tied in a series of ten to fifteen knots, and use it as a visual reminder of the boy's story. If each retreatant will take one home, prepare the small ropes before the retreat day.)

Introduction:
The grandfather of a visually challenged boy retold the saga of the boy's birth, naming ceremony, birth of his horse Rainbow, the finishing of his first horse race, and the constant struggle with the "dark curtain" in front of his eyes.

70

Through the grandfather the boy learned the meaning of *blue* by understanding *morning, sunrise, sky, song of the birds*, which the boy "[felt] in his heart."

Reading:
(Throughout the story, point out that the boy felt strong when his grandfather was with him. Draw the comparison between the grandfather's words, "You will never be alone, Boy" and the good news of God's promise to be with us always. Emphasize the similarity of "seeing" happiness in the heart and feeling God's love in nature and people.)

Discussion:

▲ Besides knots and a rope, does the object the boy and his grandfather hold on the cover of the book remind you of anything you've ever seen or used before? *(A rosary is one possibility. If many of the children haven't seen a rosary, explain that some people use a rosary to re-tell Jesus' story much like the grandfather used the knots on a rope to re-tell the boy's story.)*

▲ In this book, because the boy is unable to see with his eyes he *feels* many things in his heart using nature—wind, the bird's song, the strength of blue horses. What do you feel in your heart that you think is from God, even if you can't see it? *(Welcome suggestions from the children.)*

▲ When the rope is filled with knots, the boy will know the story by heart. What story about Jesus do you know by heart from hearing it so many times?

▲ Who in the story reminds you of Jesus? Why?

Activity 3: The Heart Room Prayer

Weave the focus of the retreat throughout the children's experience of the heart room prayer.

(Greet the children as they arrive, then invite them to sit in a circle with you. Be sure the circle is large enough that there is room between the children and they don't touch each other. Welcome the children.)

Do you have any younger brothers or sisters? Have you been around a baby for very long? Or, when were you with children who are preschool age? *(Allow time for answers.)*

As I hold up these pictures of young children, look at them and think of one way this little person is different from an adult. *(Allow time for the youngsters to look at the picture and answer the question. Try to steer the conversation to qualities of dependence and trust, simplicity, playfulness, etc.)*

We mentioned that young children trust adults. Why do you think it's important that adults be trustworthy with children? Think of examples of times that children need to depend on adults. Right now in your lives, how do you depend on the adults in your life? *(Encourage examples from the participants.)*

Let's use a game to demonstrate the importance of trust. Let's see what happens when we're able to trust someone else. *(Ask children to count off 1-2, 1-2, and pair up with a partner close by who has the other number. Pass out a paper bubble to each partner #2 and instruct them to write their names on it. The #2 participants give their bubbles to their partners and leave the room. The #1 participants hide their partner's bubbles somewhere in the room. The #2 children return to the room.)*

While you were out of the room, your partner hid your bubble somewhere in this room. Your partner is going to help you find your bubble, but he/she will not be able to use any words. All directions must be given with hand motions. Your partner wants to help you and will do everything to help you find your bubble. You must trust your partner completely. After you've found your bubble with your partner's help, come sit down over here until all have finished.

Partners #2, did you believe you were receiving trustworthy directions? *(Help the child articulate his/her feelings.)* Partners #1, how did you feel when you knew you were helping your partner find the bubbles? What did you learn about trust from this experience? It's good to know we can trust each other, isn't it? Our lives feel safe when we know we can trust people. God, too, is someone we can always trust no matter what.

God has a great way of showing us love. It's through the people in our lives we can trust. Those people who forgive us when we were sorry are like Jesus when he forgave the people he met. Those people who give us hugs and let us know we're special are like Jesus when he did the same in Galilee, Nazareth, or Jerusalem. These are the people we know we can trust because they act like Jesus.

Sometimes it takes practice recognizing *when* God is loving us. It also takes practice recognizing *how* God is showing us love. Let me help you understand this better. Can you think of someone you know who does things like Jesus would do? Someone who is kind, honest, friendly like Jesus would be? *(Encourage answers that include their peers who mirror these qualities.)*

Something in the gospel of Matthew talks about what we've been doing in our retreat today. Listen to what Matthew tells us about children, adults and Jesus. *(Read Matthew 18:1-5 slowly, emphasizing verses 3-5.)*

"About this time the disciples came to Jesus and asked him who would be the greatest in the kingdom of heaven. Jesus called a child over and had the child stand near him. Then he said: 'I promise you this, if you don't change and become like a child, you will never get into the kingdom of heaven. But if you are as humble as this child, you are the greatest in the kingdom of heaven. And when you welcome one of these children because of me, you welcome me.'"

Who did Jesus say was the most important of all? Right, a little child. But that could be a problem. Let's look at our pictures of the young children and toddlers again. How can you be like that now that you're seven, eight, nine, ten years old? Listen to what Jesus said in this sentence: "I promise you this. If you don't change and become like a child, you will never get into the kingdom of heaven." Hmmmm. That's confusing. Let's talk about this. We can't go back and be little again. Do we have to suck our thumbs again? Do we have to cry when we want something because we don't know how to talk? Do we have to begin to crawl, or forget how to ride a bike? You're right. That sounds foolish. Who remembers the qualities of little children that we talked about earlier? *(Encourage responses.)* That's right. Trusting, dependent, not showing off. That's what Jesus means about being like children. When we depend on God, or trust God, we remember God will be with us all the time. God will be with us in the people we meet.

Remember when we depended on each other to help find the bubbles? We trusted that our partners would help us, and they did. That's what Jesus is like. People can depend on Jesus. They can trust him.

I'd like to show you a way you can pray and talk with Jesus. It's important to know, though, that Jesus isn't somewhere far away. Jesus lives within each one of us, in a place deep inside. I call this place the heart room. Your heart room is a place where it's quiet, where you can go anytime you want to and place yourself in the presence of Jesus, your friend.

It helps me to close my eyes and tune out any sounds. Let's all close our eyes. Don't worry that you'll be the only one. I'll keep my own eyes open to make sure it's safe for everyone. All of us have our eyes closed so we won't be distracted.

I'll lead you now through some helps for praying in our heart room. First, take a deep breath to help you relax. Fine. Let's take another deep breath. We all have our eyes closed. As I lead you through this type of prayer please use my suggestions to make pictures in your mind.

Let's imagine we're outside in a park. Jesus is sitting with you under a large tree. Feel the breeze and the warmth of the sun. *(Pause.)* Listen to the sounds of birds and insects. *(Pause.)* Picture yourself sitting near Jesus. What does he look like? What color is his hair? Is it curly? Straight? Long? Short? *(Pause.)* Now look at his face. Is he smiling? How does he look at you? *(Pause.)* When you look at his face do you feel peaceful, happy? What are your feelings when you look at Jesus' face? How is Jesus dressed? What color is his skin?

We can tell Jesus whatever we would like because he has shown us we can trust him. What would you like to say to Jesus? In our heart room, we don't have to worry that we might say the wrong thing or that Jesus might not understand us. Knowing we're with such an incredibly good friend, let's take a minute to talk with Jesus right now. I'll stop for a short time and you can tell Jesus whatever you would like. Jesus might also want to say something to you. So listen... *(Wait 60 seconds.)*

It's time to go now. Say goodbye to Jesus in whatever way you'd like. Wave, hug him, or say some simple words. *(Pause.)* Tell Jesus you'll come back to your heart room again. *(Pause.)* Now imagine yourself walking back to our room here. *(Pause.)*

When you're ready, please open your eyes.

Sometimes it helps to look back on what happened in prayer in our heart rooms. How did you feel when you were in your heart room? Did you have an easy time talking to Jesus? Do you believe he heard you? Did Jesus say anything to you? Sometimes we hear Jesus and sometimes we don't. That's natural. *(Allow children time to share.)*

Now that you've had a chance to talk to Jesus in your heart room, you can do this any time you want. There's no place off-limits for talking to Jesus, no time that's too early or too late. You can repeat this prayer anytime you'd like to talk to Jesus. The heart room has been a good, peaceful place, hasn't it?

Thank you, Jesus, for teaching us that we can depend on you and trust you.

Remember what we did here in our retreat. I hope you have many happy and prayerful times with Jesus in your heart room when you pray this way again.

Snack

root beer floats

Adult-Child Sharing Time

After the adult session, parents or adult retreat leaders join their children in the snack room to begin their sharing time. If weather permits, retreatants can go outside for a nature walk. If not, they might want to find a corner to sit in, take a walk through the church, spread out blankets throughout the room, or even create forts out of blankets to sit in for privacy. We allow approximately twenty minutes for adult-child sharing time, asking all participants to return to the gathering room at the allotted time for our closing.

The questions on p. 214 can facilitate adult-child sharing.

If time remains, parents or adult leaders can help children compose a song to a familiar tune, using the concepts of the retreat.

For example:
(To the tune of "Row, Row, Row Your Boat")

> Trust, trust, trust in God,
> Jesus says to us.
> When we trust we will find God
> In people that we meet.

(To accommodate children who are not auditory learners, print the lyrics of each song on a large poster board and display.)

Closing Prayer

The children can close with song, teaching each other the lyrics their group composed. Following the prayer of joyful song, an adult facilitator leads the children in the following litany:

Adult:	I invite all of you to join me in prayer. First, I'll say something to God for all of us. Then you say, "That's Good News."
Adult:	Loving God, we gather in your name. You are here with us now.
Children:	That's Good News.
Adult:	Loving God, you loved us first.
Children:	That's Good News.
Adult:	Loving God, you let us see your love through the kind people we meet.
Children:	That's Good News.

Adult: Loving God, it takes practice recognizing when and how you are making your love known to us.

Children: That's Good News.

Adult: So, loving God, we're going to start looking for your love.

Children: That's Good News.

Invite children to join hands and say the Our Father.

5-The Great Commandment Retreat

(John 15:15-16; 1 John 4:19; Matthew 22:37-39)

If giving a family retreat that includes three- to six-year-olds, coordinate with the retreat entitled "Valentine's Day" from *Parent-Child Retreats: Spiritual Experiences for Children Ages 3-6 and Their Parents* (Living the Good News, 1997).

Focus

What seven- to ten-year-old hasn't been the victim of a bully, boss, or braggart? Some of the children on this retreat have resorted to those tactics themselves. Bullying assaults the victim's self-esteem; bragging originates from an undeveloped sense of self. The Great Commandment invites us to approach people from a different stance: love. The love Jesus speaks of consists of three intertwined parts: love of God, neighbor and self.

Jesus instructed us to love *ourselves*, but children more often hear how they should love others. "Be nice," "Share," "Don't shout," are common admonitions when children attempt to test their importance. Later, their peers tell them to stop showing off. Achieving humility—that is, loving what is good about ourselves, yet embracing our shadow side as well—is a tricky endeavor for most of us. Children need adult guidance in this delicate development. If children don't love themselves and appreciate their own gifts, they have difficulty loving others, and they have difficulty being open to the friendship of Jesus.

We want children to understand that we love even when someone isn't perfect. When we say someone bothers us because of something they do or say, this doesn't mean our love is less. Children can practice speaking about people in this way, too. Their friends, parents, or teachers can "drive them crazy;" nonetheless, they love these important people in their lives.

The focus of the retreat can be summarized in four statements:
▲ Jesus told us to love God, each other, and ourselves.
▲ Our relationship with ourselves and our relationship with others mirror our relationship with God.
▲ Loving ourselves might seem like bragging, but it's not. We can't love each other if we don't love ourselves.
▲ The people we like to be around—the ones who are the most like Jesus—are people who love themselves.

Preparations Before the Retreat

1. Meet as a team to pray, read, discuss, understand, and interiorize the focus and scriptural basis for the retreat.
2. Discern which team members will be responsible for the gathering presentation, each of the three children's activities, and the optional adult retreat section.
3. If this is to be a family retreat, choose an adult retreat topic from the section entitled Outlines for Parent Sessions (pp. 163-184). If parents will not be present, prepare a letter to send home for parent-child follow-up enrichment (p. 190).
4. Divide preparation responsibilities. Use the gifts of the community to lighten the load. Parents, teenagers, school children, and senior citizens can all help prepare.

Make nametags in three colors.

Collect materials for the environment.
Bible
picture of Jesus
sample souvenir

book for story session
bulletin board or poster with the words "The Great Commandment" to which the mirrors will be added after the retreat

Prepare the retreat souvenir (p. 82).
First, gather materials for each retreatant:
▲ pencil to keep
▲ scissors
▲ reproduced pocket page inserts
▲ small contemporary picture of Jesus to glue on the cover (optional)
▲ two 12" x 18" sheets plus one 9" x 12" sheet of construction paper, assorted colors

For retreatants to share:
▲ markers
▲ glue and stapler (one for each two retreatants working in a group)
▲ several rolls of cellophane tape

Second, do the advance preparation.
1. Reproduce the blackline master inserts for pocket pages. (See pp. 206-210.)
2. Fold the 9" x 12" sheets up from the bottom two inches.
3. Staple each end of the fold shut to form a pocket. Students will use this folded page as a guide when making other pockets.
4. Make a sample to use as a demonstration at the retreat. Write and draw on its pocket pages and decorate its cover so it looks like a finished product.

Locate the story.
Obtain *Love You Forever* by Robert Munsch (Willowdale, Ontario, Canada: Firefly Books, 1986). If unable to locate the first choice of literature, substitute *I'm In Charge of Celebrations* by Byrd Baylor (New York: Simon and Schuster, 1995). If using the second choice, cut out one four-inch paper heart shape for each retreatant and change the letter to parents.

Prepare for the gathering presentation.

Make 3 cardboard hand mirrors covered in foil bearing these messages:

Mirror 1: The more we know God loves us

Mirror 2: The more we love ourselves

Mirror 3: The better we love other people

Become familiar with the heart room prayer (p. 86).

Gather materials: For each retreatant, one heart-shaped slip of paper, a pencil, an 8 1/2" x 11" paper cut into the shape of a T-shirt (see p. 206), and colored markers. Optional: a display of real T-shirts with different messages on them.

Purchase groceries and prepare the snack.

▲ knotted pretzels or frozen round waffles

▲ syrup

▲ juice or milk

Duplicate the Adult-Child Sharing Form (p. 214) or letter to parents (p. 190).

Preparations the Day of the Retreat

1. Gather as a team and pray.
2. Set out nametags and safety pins or tape (*warning: no straight pins or strings*). Have exactly as many nametags as retreatants, and equal numbers of nametags for each color group.
3. Have each retreat team member wear a different colored nametag. This will later help the children divide into groups for their activities.
4. On top of a piano or table, create the environment in the gathering room with an arrangement that reflects the theme of the retreat. Include the book that will be read during the retreat, a sample of the souvenir the children will make, a picture of Jesus, a Bible, and a bulletin board or poster with the words "The Great Commandment" to which the mirrors will be added after the retreat.
5. Gather all the materials for the retreat souvenir and set out on tables in the room that will be used for this activity.
6. Spread out so that at least one team member is greeting the retreatants as they arrive, one is bringing retreatants (and parents) to the gathering room, one is waiting in the gathering room, and one is directing parents and younger siblings to the nursery.
7. Begin the retreat by warmly greeting the retreatants, then introducing the team members.

Gathering Presentation

Who knows what a bully is? I need to see what a bully acts like. Could two of you show me? *(Allow time for role playing.)*

How about two more? Can you show us another way bullies act?

Here's a little secret: Do you know that bullies are people who don't love themselves? That's true. And because of this they find it hard to love other people. That's a strange thing about people, but it's really true. Bullies try to make us think they're the best and strongest, but they act that way because they don't feel lovable.

Who has ever been annoyed by someone who brags a lot?

Raise your hand if you know someone who's bossy.

Who can show us what people who brag a lot act like? *(Allow time for role playing.)*

Who would like to act like a bossy person? *(Allow time for role playing.)*

Here's another thing I want you to know: People who don't love themselves often don't think other people love them and sometimes wonder if God even loves them. *(Hold up two of the mirrors facing each other.)* It's like these mirrors. If I look into a mirror and see the goodness of Jesus in my own face, then I know how lovable I am, and I love both myself and Jesus. But if I don't see the goodness of Jesus in myself, then, to make myself feel more lovable, I try to make everybody think I'm the strongest and the best. Then I'm not doing a good job of loving others.

Listen to these words from the Bible. *(Read Mt. 22:37-39 and 1 Jn. 4:19.)*

"Love the Lord your God with all your heart, soul, and mind. This is the first and most important commandment. The second most important commandment is like this one. And it is, 'Love others as much as you love yourself'" (Mt. 22:37-39).

"We love because God loved us first" (1 Jn. 4:19).

This is why Jesus spoke about love so much. He knew how important it was to know God loves us. The more we know God loves us, the more we love ourselves, and the better we love other people. It works the other way, too: the more we love ourselves, the more we know God loves us, and the better we love other people.

What I just told you is what Jesus told us during his life on earth, and it's so important I'd like us all to say it again. In fact, I'd like us to *see* how amazing these words are.

(Solicit volunteers to hold three foil-covered cardboard hand mirrors, each one posted with one of these three sentences:

The more we know God loves us.

The more we love ourselves.

The better we love other people.)

Each person is holding one of the three parts of the Great Commandment that Jesus gave us: Love God and love your neighbor as yourself. No matter how we arrange and rearrange the parts of the commandment, it still shows us how important it is to love God, love ourselves, and love each other. Now, when I say "Scramble" I'd like our three mirror-holders to move around this area and place themselves in a new position.

Ready? Scramble! *(Each time the children reposition themselves, invite the rest of the children to read the cards in their new order.)*

Jesus spent his life showing us how to be loving people. Let's start noticing the happiest people we know. Maybe it's your mom or dad, or an aunt or a neighbor. Maybe it's one of your friends. Or maybe *you're* one of the most loving people you know. Let's notice if these people love God, love themselves, and love other people. The people we like to be around—the people who are most like Jesus—are people who love themselves.

Children's Activities

The following three children's activities run simultaneously, and the children rotate through them until they've been to all three.

Activity 1: Art as Prayer—Retreat Souvenir

The retreatants will make a Heart Room Scrapbook, a five-pocket book for retreat mementos, as a way to preserve and internalize the focus of the retreat after they return home.

As the children make their scrapbooks, talk about the focus of the retreat (p. 78).

Gather participants around the materials table to create Heart Room Scrapbooks.

1. Participants select two colors of construction paper and one smaller pre-folded paper, and place them horizontally in front of them.

2. Children make pockets by folding each large sheet from the bottom the same depth as the pre-made half sheet sample.

3. Retreatants staple both ends of the pockets shut.

4. They fold the left side to touch the right side and crease the middle fold firmly to make folders.

5. Children place one "folder" inside the other with the center folds matched up vertically, then insert the half-sheet sample with its left side touching the center fold.

6. Children close the book and staple it three times vertically in the center to secure the three pieces of paper.

7. Leader checks to make sure every retreatant has a five-pocket folder.

8. Leader distributes the insert pocket pages (pp. 206-210) and pencils and encourages retreatants to write and draw in them throughout the retreat, and to collect items to glue in as follow-up at home.

9. Participants complete the cover, gluing on their small picture of Jesus.

Announce to the children: It's almost time to move to your next prayer session. Please help me get ready for the next group by setting up the table the way it was when you arrived. *(To the final group, give directions about how to put supplies away.)*

Activity 2: Story as Prayer

Story: *Love You Forever* by Robert Munsch (Willowdale, Ontario, Canada: Firefly Books, 1986)

As the children listen to and discuss the literature, talk about the focus of the retreat (p.78).

Greet the children.

(As the retreatants enter the room, designate a space where they can put their belongings, then invite them to sit where they can see the pictures of the book.)

Raise your hand if you've heard this story before. Wonderful. If you have, let's not tell the others what happens so they can enjoy their experience, too.

This is a time of prayer. Let's get ready to listen to what God wants us to hear in this story. Are you in a comfortable position? Let's all take a deep breath and let it out a little at a time.

Introduce the story.

This story tells of a parent who loves her child, even when he does annoying things, and even after he's grown up and has moved away. Because this boy has known love all his life, he passes love to his own child in the same way. Listen for the person in the story that is like Jesus—someone who loves even when the person they love is not perfect. We'll talk at the end of the book about who you think that is. *(Invite the children to join in the refrain, "I'll love you forever, I'll like you for always. As long as I'm living, my baby you'll be.")*

Read the story, taking ample time to show the pictures.

(Using voice intonations, pauses, and a prayerful sense of awe, read the book aloud. Allow time for children to be touched by the words as well as the illustrations. At the conclusion, close the book gently and allow a moment of "think time.")

Talk about the story.

▲ What part of the story did you especially like?
▲ Who was the character who reminded you of Jesus? In what way?
▲ Who remembers what the Great Commandment asks of us? *(To love God, other people, and ourselves.)* Did the mother and child in this book live by the Great Commandment? How?
▲ God has told us God will be with us always. What similar message did the parent give the child in this story? *(I'll love you forever.)*
▲ Do you think the mother loved herself? How about the child? How do you know?

84

▲ Our relationship with ourselves and our relationship with others mirrors our relationship with God. How did the mother and child mirror God's relationship with us?

(Hold up the book with the cover facing the children.) When you're telling your family about the book you read during the retreat today, remember this title. Let's say it together: *Love You Forever.*

Announce to the children: Now it's time to move to the next retreat session. Be sure to take any of your belongings with you on your way out. Let's walk together.

Alternate Story

If the first choice of literature for this session is unavailable, substitute *I'm In Charge of Celebrations* by Byrd Baylor (New York: Simon and Schuster, 1995).

Introduction:
A desert dweller celebrated what mattered most to her—dust devils, rainbows, green clouds, coyotes, falling stars, and "New Year"—the coming of spring. Being "in charge of celebrations" kept the main character very busy as she was keenly aware of all God's creation around her.

Reading:
(Throughout the story, help the children discern great praise for God as the desert dweller celebrates God's creation. When we spend our time admiring things in nature, we give glory to God. We are telling God, "Hooray! Good job, I love the _____ you made."

With family and classmates, too, we praise God when we notice something that makes us want to whistle, hum, or sing their praises. We thank God for the gift they are to us.)

Discussion:
▲ What celebration mentioned in this story made you want to join in?
▲ Create a celebration day of your own and tell us about it. *(Examples to get retreatants started: first snow of the season day, all the leaves off the trees day, the best beach day, brother or sister day, the most fun with a friend day, store clerk kindness day.)*
▲ Write on a heart shape what you would say if you could create just one new celebration day. (Example: Love Day—For all those who've been kind to me.) Put it in a place at home to remind you to celebrate God's love.
▲ Is there someone or something in this story that reminded you of Jesus?

Activity 3: The Heart Room Prayer

(Greet the children as they arrive, then invite them to sit in a circle with you. Be sure the circle is large enough that there is room between the children and they don't touch each other.)

I'm so glad you are all able to be here today. We're going to be thinking about Valentine's Day in a little different way. What is the symbol we usually see around February 14? That's right, hearts—and more hearts! What does the symbol of the heart mean? Yes, love.

Love is so important to God that Jesus told us there are only two commandments: Love God, and love others as much as you love yourself. Does it seem kind of strange to you to hear Jesus tell us to love ourselves? It might sound conceited. But when we think about it, it really isn't conceited at all. Instead, loving ourselves means recognizing the wonderful gifts we've all received from God. Loving ourselves also means being smart enough to know what our strong points really are.

I'm going to give each of you a slip of paper. Please write down two good qualities or talents that God has given you. Think about what qualities people admire about you. Please don't put your name on the paper, just the two gifts you choose to think about.

(Pass the paper and pencils. Include yourself and write your gifts while the children are writing theirs. After a few minutes, collect the papers and pencils.)

Listen as I read the list of gifts that come from our circle. Are there gifts on the list that you could use to describe someone here or that you yourself have? *(Encourage a discussion of the uniqueness of those present. Point out that our gifts complement the gifts of others. What another can do, we may not be able to do, yet pooling our gifts with others' gifts helps everyone.)*

(Shift the discussion to the way T-shirts are used to communicate various messages. If you have an assortment, display them before the children.) Let's see what kinds of messages these T-shirts carry. Hmmmm. I see some T-shirts with team logos. What do you see? *(Try to cover the gamut from rock groups to tourist spots to cartoon characters. Lead the children in a discussion of the various messages.)*

A Valentine message might also appear on a T-shirt. A T-shirt covered with hearts or cupids is surely a Valentine's message, but *any* message of love is a Valentine's message. We get a clue of God's strong Valentine's message to us in the gospel of Matthew. Listen especially to the part about the two commandments of love.

86

(Read Matthew 22:36-39.)

"'Teacher, what is the most important commandment in the law?' Jesus answered: 'Love the Lord your God with all your heart, soul, and mind. This is the first and most important commandment. The second most important commandment is like this one. And it is, 'Love others as much as you love yourself.'"

What did you hear about love? That's right. Jesus told us to love God, and to love our neighbor as we love ourselves.

(Explain to the retreatants that they will each get a cut-out in the shape of a T-shirt. Ask them to put their name on the front of the T-shirt. Invite the participants to find a place in the room to leave their T-shirt. Make sure the shirts are spread out and that there is room between them. Then invite the children back to the circle and give each one a marker.)

Jesus had described the kind of love God expects from us. Jesus said we must love God and love our neighbor as ourselves. Let's walk around the room now and write a message of love on each of the T-shirts. When you look at the name on each T-shirt, think of something you could write that would let that person know you care about him or her. If the person has a particular quality you admire, write about that. If this person does something well, let them know. If you don't know a person very well, write a good wish for them on their T-shirt. Even if you don't like a person, write a good wish for them. You can sign your name or write your initials if you want. *(Allow 5 minutes for the T-shirt autographing, occasionally reminding the children of how much time they have to finish signing all the shirts. Circulate around the room writing messages on children's T-shirts. Make sure every shirt has at least some messages. After five minutes, invite the children to pick up their own T-shirt and return to the circle. Allow a few minutes to silently read the notes on their T-shirts.)*

I'd like to show you a way you can pray and talk with Jesus. It's important to know, though, that Jesus isn't somewhere far away. Jesus lives within each one of us, in a place deep inside. I call this place the heart room. Your heart room is a place where it's quiet, where you can go anytime you want to and place yourself in the presence of Jesus, your friend.

It helps me to close my eyes and tune out any sounds. Let's all close our eyes. Don't worry that you'll be the only one. I'll keep my own eyes open to make sure it's safe for everyone. All of us have our eyes closed so we won't be distracted.

I'll lead you now through some helps in learning how to pray this way. First, take a deep breath to help you relax. Fine. Let's take another deep breath. We all have our eyes closed. As I lead you through this type of prayer please use my suggestions to make pictures in your mind.

You're sitting in an ordinary room that's familiar to you. Is it your bedroom? Your living room? Imagine what sights you see, what sounds you hear, what scents you smell. *(Pause.)* Someone just walked into the room, our heart room. It's Jesus. *(Pause.)* What does he look like? What color is his hair? Is it curly? Straight? Long? Short? *(Pause.)* Now look at his face. Is he smiling? How does he look at you? *(Pause.)* When you look at his face do you feel peaceful, happy? What are your feelings when you look at Jesus' face? How is Jesus dressed? What color is his skin?

Jesus sits down next to you. *(Pause.)* Make yourself comfortable next to Jesus. He's there just for you. What would you like to say to Jesus? In our heart room, we don't have to worry that we might say the wrong thing or that Jesus might not understand us. Knowing we're with such an incredibly good friend, let's take a minute to talk with Jesus right now. I'll stop for a short time and you can tell Jesus whatever you would like. Jesus might also want to say something to you. So listen... *(Wait 60 seconds.)*

It's time to go now. Say goodbye to Jesus in whatever way you'd like. Wave, hug him, or say some simple words. *(Pause.)* Tell Jesus you'll come back to your heart room again. *(Pause.)* Now imagine yourself walking back to our room here. *(Pause.)*

When you're ready, please open your eyes.

Sometimes it helps to look back on what happened in prayer in our heart rooms.

How did you feel when you were in your heart room? Did you have an easy time talking to Jesus? Do you believe he heard you? Did Jesus say anything to you? Sometimes we hear Jesus and sometimes we don't. That's natural. *(Allow children time to share as they desire.)*

Now that you've had a chance to talk to Jesus in your heart room, you can do this anytime you want. There's no place off-limits for talking to Jesus, no time that's too early or too late. This prayer can be repeated anytime you feel you'd like to talk to Jesus. It's been a good, peaceful place, hasn't it?

Remember what we did here in our retreat. I hope you have many happy and prayerful times with Jesus in your heart room whenever you decide to pray this way again.

Snack

knotted pretzels *(Point out that pretzels are shaped like hearts.)*

or

round waffles and syrup *(Cut out a small wedge to make the waffles heart-shaped.)*

Adult-Child Sharing Time

After the adult session, parents or adult retreat leaders join their children in the snack room to begin their sharing time. If weather permits, retreatants can go outside for a nature walk. If not, they might want to find a corner to sit in, take a walk through the church, spread out blankets throughout the room, or even create forts out of blankets to sit in for privacy. We allow approximately twenty minutes for adult-child sharing time, asking all participants to return to the gathering room at the allotted time for our closing.

The questions on p. 214 can facilitate adult-child sharing.

If time remains, parents or adult leaders can help children compose a song to a familiar tune, using the concepts of the retreat.

For example:
(To the tune of "On Top of Old Smokey")

> I wake in the morning
> And look in the mirror.
> I see a reflection
> Of Jesus, who's near.
> I see Jesus smiling
> When I look at me.
> The one in the mirror
> Is God's plan for me.

(To accommodate children who are not auditory learners, print the lyrics of each song on a large poster board and display.)

Closing Prayer

The children can close with song, teaching each other the lyrics their group composed. Following the prayer of joyful song, an adult facilitator leads the children in the following litany:

Adult: I invite all of you to join me in prayer. First, I'll say something to Jesus for all of us. Then you say, "We love God, ourselves, and each other."

Adult: Our friend Jesus, you told us to love God, ourselves, and each other.

Children: We love God, ourselves, and each other.

Adult: Our friend Jesus, when we love ourselves, we're not bragging. We can't love others if we don't love ourselves.

Children: We love God, ourselves, and each other.

Adult: Our friend Jesus, how we love ourselves and each other mirrors the way we love you.

Children: We love God, ourselves, and each other.

Adult: Our friend Jesus, the people we like being around the most are like you.

Children: We love God, ourselves, and each other.

Adult: Our friend Jesus, the people we enjoy being around the most love God, themselves, and each other.

Children: We love God, ourselves, and each other.

Invite children to join hands and say the Our Father.

6-Come As You Are Retreat

(Luke 2:41-52; Psalm 142:2-3; Psalm 44:3-7)

If giving a family retreat that includes three- to six-year-olds, coordinate with the retreat entitled "Mother's Day/Father's Day" from *Parent-Child Retreats: Spiritual Experiences for Children Ages 3-6 and Their Parents* (Living the Good News, 1997).

Focus

Integrity is one goal of the spiritual life, but the transformation towards authenticity is a great spiritual challenge. Children's lives are replete with demands to be better, always improving their performance in sports and school. Later, careers will have similar demands, as most adults can attest. No wonder it's difficult to believe that God accepts us exactly the way we are. Few other people ever have.

Transformation into our authentic self begins with understanding our relationship with God. How easy it is, given our real life models, to apologize about ourselves before this great God. Many adults have brought a pattern of distance from God into adulthood. But our children can be free of this barrier. We remind children that they can say anything to God. No amount of anger, sadness, or worry will make God angry at us. The psalmists seemed to know this.

We also examine our actions. Children make many mistakes as they grow to maturity, and no one understands this better than God. We can do nothing that will make Jesus abandon us. Even when we think of the person in our life who loves us the most, we can be assured there's someone who loves us even more: Jesus. Jesus takes us as we are. His love has the power to heal us in body, mind, and spirit.

We help children to love themselves. In order to do this, they must understand how important they are to God. God initiated a relationship of intimacy, has promised to be with us always, and, therefore, is the most loyal friend we have.

As children grow secure in their relationship with God, sure that their actions won't keep them away from God's love, and strong in their sense of self as lovable beings, they will be better able to interiorize the meaning of the words from *The Velveteen Rabbit*: "Real isn't how you're made, it's what happens when you are loved."

The focus of the retreat can be summarized in three statements:
▲ There's nothing we can do or say that will make Jesus go away.
▲ Jesus loves us at least as much as the person who loves us the most.[1]
▲ We can share all our feelings with God—angry, glad, sad, or scared—just as Job and the psalmists did.

Preparations Before the Retreat

1. Meet as a team to pray, read, discuss, understand, and interiorize the focus and scriptural basis for the retreat.
2. Discern which team members will be responsible for the gathering presentation, each of the three children's activities, and the adult retreat section, if there is one.
3. If this is to be a family retreat, choose an adult retreat topic from the section entitled Outlines for Parent Sessions (pp. 163-184). If parents will not be

present, prepare a letter to send home for parent-child follow-up enrichment (p. 191).

4. Divide preparation responsibilities. Use the gifts from the community to lighten the load. Parents, teenagers, school children, and senior citizens can all help prepare.

Make nametags in three colors.

Collect materials for the environment.
Bible
picture of Jesus
sample souvenir
book for story session
pictures of children showing different feelings
bulletin board or poster with the words "Jesus loves us as we are."

Prepare the retreat souvenir (p. 96).
First, gather materials.

For each retreatant:
▲ black construction paper, 18" x 12" (half as many sheets as retreatants)
▲ 3" x 5" unlined notecards (3 per child)
▲ scissors

For retreatants to share:
▲ several hole punches
▲ staplers
▲ cellophane tape
▲ glue (one for every two retreatants)
▲ colored pencils/fine-tipped markers/crayons

Second, do the advance preparation.
1. Cut black paper into 6" x 18" strips.
2. Make a sample souvenir.

Locate the story.
Obtain *The Velveteen Rabbit* by Margery Williams (New York: Scholastic, 1990). If unable to locate the first literature choice, substitute *The Relatives Came* by Cynthia Rylant (New York: Scholastic, 1993). If using the alternate book, bring pictures of multigenerational crowds being friendly with one another and change the letter to parents.

Prepare for the gathering presentation.

Locate a punching bag or make one from balloons suspended by a string.

Blow up enough balloons for each child *(plus several extras, in case of popping)*, tie strings to them, and make a bouquet.

Become familiar with the heart room prayer (p. 99).

Gather materials: one sheet of newsprint for each child, container of crayons, baby oil.

Purchase groceries and prepare the snack.

▲ gingerbread people

▲ milk or juice

Duplicate the Adult-Child Sharing Form (p. 214) or letter to parents (p. 191).

Preparations the Day of the Retreat

1. Gather as a team and pray.
2. Set out nametags and safety pins or tape *(warning: no straight pins or strings)*. Have exactly as many nametags as retreatants, and equal numbers of nametags for each color group.
3. Have each retreat team member wear a different colored nametag. This will later help the children divide into groups for their activities.
4. On top of a piano or table, create the environment in the gathering room with an arrangement that reflects the theme of the retreat. Include the book that will be read during the retreat, a sample of the souvenir the children will make, a picture of Jesus, a Bible, pictures of children showing different feelings, and the bulletin board or poster with the words "Jesus loves us just as we are."
5. Gather all the materials for the retreat souvenir and set out on tables in the room that will be used for this activity.
6. Spread out so that at least one team member is greeting the retreatants as they arrive, one is bringing retreatants (and parents) to the gathering room, one is waiting in the gathering room, and one is directing parents and younger siblings to the nursery.
7. Begin the retreat by warmly greeting the retreatants, then introducing the team members.

Gathering Presentation

You know what this is? *(If it's a real punching bag, the children will know; if us-*

ing a balloon punching bag, they'll have to use their imaginations. Retreat leader may want to pantomime its use.)

That's right. This is a punching bag, and I use it when I'm really angry or sad or scared. I punch it—like this. *(Punch bag while shouting expressions of anger, sadness, or fear.)*

Sometimes this helps me feel better, but I want to share a surprise with you that I found in the Bible. Listen to this:

(Say this adaptation of Psalm 142:2-3 while hitting the punching bag: "I tell you all of my worries and my troubles, and whenever I feel low, you are there to guide me.") Hey, God. I have a complaint.

(Say this adaptation of Psalm 44:3-7 while hitting the punching bag. "Their strength and weapons were not what won the land and gave them victory! You loved them and fought with your powerful arm and your shining glory. You are my God and King, and you give victory to the people of Jacob. By your great power, we knocked our enemies down and stomped on them. I don't depend on my arrows or my sword to save me. But you saved us from our hateful enemies and you put them to shame.") Way to go, God! You helped us smash our enemies!

(Invite 6 children to take turns hitting the punching bag while leader suggests these phrases: Okay, God. I'm ready to talk. *(Child punches bag.)* Things are hard for me now. *(Child punches bag.)* My mom yelled at me. *(Child punches bag.)* My best friend just moved away. *(Child punches bag.)* My big brother won't let me play with him. *(Child punches bag.)* I got kicked on the playground. *(Child punches bag.)* Take that *(Child punches bag)* and that *(Child punches bag)* and that *(Child punches bag)* and that *(Child punches bag)* and that *(Child punches bag)* and that. *(Child punches bag).*

Are you as surprised as I was that people really talk to God like that? God wants us to be friends, and promised to be with us always—even when we're angry or sad, glad or scared. The people we read about in the Bible understood that. There's nothing we can say or do that will make Jesus go away from us even when we do wrong or hurtful things. The people we read about in the Bible felt so close to God that they knew they would feel better talking to God about their feelings than if they punched a punching bag.

We're free to talk to Jesus, too, no matter how we feel. We're all part of God's family. God is loving to us like a mother or father is, like an aunt or uncle, or like a grandparent. In fact, God loves us *even more* than the person who loves us the most.

Let's stop for a minute and think about the person we think loves us the most. *(Pause.)* Think about how that person shows you love. Now I'm going to tell you that Jesus loves you even more. Some adults and friends love us, but get angry at us when we make mistakes. But Jesus never does. Even more than the person who loves us the most, Jesus understands why we get sad, scared, or angry. Jesus takes us as we are.

This retreat today is an opportunity to spend special time with our friend Jesus. I'd like to give you each a punching bag to remind you that you can say anything to Jesus and he won't go away. *(Hand out balloons on strings.)* Let's practice punching. *(Leader and children hold onto their strings and punch their balloons, letting the noise calm down naturally.)*

Let's do one more thing with these balloons. Let's all shout, "Thank you for loving us just as we are," then throw our balloons as high as we can. Ready? All together: Thank you for loving us just as we are! *(Wait for the commotion to die down and for the children to retrieve their balloons, then instruct the children to sit down quietly and listen.)*

We have some fun activities to do now. Let me show you what we'll be doing. *(Show the children the souvenir and story, and tell them they'll also be talking to Jesus.)* Now look at the color of your nametag. *(Have the children leave the room with the team leader who has the same colored nametag.)*

Children's Activities
The following three children's activities run simultaneously, and the children rotate through them until they've been to all three.

Activity 1: Art as Prayer—Retreat Souvenir
The retreatants will create a paper filmstrip to record their retreat adventure with pictures. Pictures will show their prayerful response to the story, heart room activity, and art.

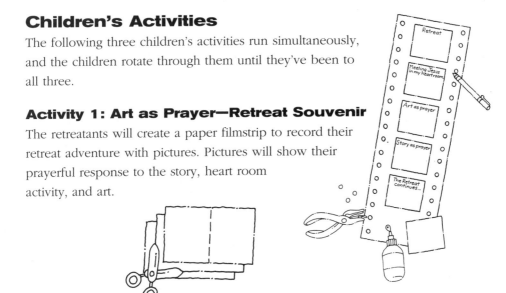

As the children make their filmstrip picture frames, talk about the focus of the retreat (p.92).

Gather retreatants around the materials table where each has two black paper strips, three file cards, and a scissors.

1. Children cut the 3" x 5" cards in half (see drawing) to make two frames on the film. They place the cards vertically on the black paper background so that some of the black sticks off the side to make a bit of a frame.
2. Children make holes with a hole punch in a vertical line along the edge to create a more realistic look.
3. Retreatants write "Retreat" and the year on the first white card.
4. In smaller letters, participants write "Meeting Jesus in my heart room" on the second card; "Art as Prayer" on the third card; and "Story as Prayer" on the fourth card.
5. If retreatants have been to the Story or Heart Room Prayer sessions, they should spend time illustrating those now. If those sessions are still to come, write the words now and draw pictures later after you experience them.
6. To prepare for parent-child sharing of the retreat at home, children glue a fifth and sixth card at the end. Label card 5, "The retreat continues...." Children write their names on card 6.

Announce to the children: It's almost time to move to your next prayer session. Please help me get ready for the next group by setting up the table the way it was when you arrived. *(To the final group, give directions about how to put supplies away.)*

Activity 2: Story as Prayer
Story: *The Velveteen Rabbit* by Margery Williams (New York: Scholastic, 1990)

As the children listen to and discuss the literature, talk about the focus of the retreat (p. 92).

Greet the children.
(As retreatants enter the room, designate a space where they can put their belongings, then invite them to sit where they can see the pictures of the book.)

Raise your hand if you've heard this story before. Wonderful. If you have, let's not tell the others what happens so they can enjoy their experience, too.

This is a time of prayer. Let's get ready to listen to what God wants us to hear in this story. Are you in a comfortable position? Let's all take a deep breath and let it out a little at a time.

Introduce the story.

In this classic tale, a stuffed rabbit belonged to a family for generations and was loved until it looked shabby. Its greatest desire was to become real. Once someone is Real, the rabbit learned, he or she can't be ugly except to people who don't understand. Listen for how the Skin Horse in the nursery explains what it means to be Real.

Listen also for the important words of the magic fairy, who takes care of playthings children have loved. Her words always remind me of words God might have said to your parents when they first saw you: "You must be very kind to [this child] and teach him or her all he or she needs to know, for [this child] is going to live with you for ever and ever."

Read the story, allowing ample time to show the pictures.
(Using voice intonations, pauses, and a prayerful sense of awe, read the book aloud. Allow time for children to be touched by the words as well as the illustrations. At the conclusion, close the book gently and allow a moment of "think time.")

Talk about the story.

▲ What did "being Real" mean to the Skin Horse? *("Real isn't how you're made, it's what happens when you are loved.")*

▲ What does happen when we're loved? Have you ever been kind to someone to whom no one else was usually kind? What happened?

▲ The rabbit asked if it hurt to be Real. What did the Skin Horse answer? *(Sometimes, but when you are Real you don't mind being hurt.)* What do you think about that?

▲ What does it mean to be Real with God? *(Jesus wants us to know we can share all our feelings with God—even when we're sad, scared, lonely, worried, and feeling left out. That's part of being Real with God. Our realness comes from being loved by God just as we are. We don't look shabby to God.)*

(Hold up the book with the cover facing the children.) When you're telling your family about the book you read during the retreat today, remember this title. Let's say it together: *The Velveteen Rabbit.*

Announce to the children: Now it's time to move to the next retreat session. Be sure to take any of your belongings with you on your way out. Let's walk together.

98

Alternate Story

If the first choice of literature for this session is unavailable, substitute *The Relatives Came* by Cynthia Rylant (New York: Scholastic, 1993).

Introduction:

An extended family who lived in two different states anticipated, celebrated, then remembered the joys of being together. They arrived in the summer and stayed for weeks—hugging, eating, talking, and laughing together. They could talk to each other about anything and everything. It was hard to tell who was the person in the story who loved the most.

Reading:

(Throughout the story, point out how everyone was busy being present to each other in love. The pictures tell at least half the story in this book. Linger on them to fully appreciate the depth of feeling those folks had for one another. This is a multigenerational family. Use specific words like grandma, uncle, cousin, niece, and grandchild when exploring the pictures.)

Discussion:

▲ What do you think their "quiet talk" was about when they were in 2's and 3's? *(Point out that people who love each other can safely share all feelings with each other.)*

▲ To fully understand the impact of "all that breathing in the house," let's all lie down for a moment and breathe a little louder than usual. How would you feel about sharing your room with six extra people? How did the people in the story like it? *(Just fine. They were excited about being together.)*

▲ Have you ever had a family reunion, large or small, such as the one described in this story? How was it the same? Different?

▲ Does anything in this story remind you of the event when Jesus was lost in the temple? *(Find pictures depicting multigenerational crowds traveling a long distance, being friendly with each other, where children are not only with their own parents, and point out the similarities with the story of Jesus in Luke 2:41-52.)*

▲ What feelings might the folks in this story have that they could share with God? *(Anticipation, worry, thankfulness, joy, excitement, tiredness, sadness...)*

▲ Who in this story was like Jesus?

Activity 3: The Heart Room Prayer

Weave the focus of the retreat throughout the children's experience of the heart room prayer.

(Greet the children as they arrive, then invite them to sit in a circle with you. Be sure the circle is large enough that there is room between the children and they don't touch each other. Welcome the children.)

Today we're going to spend some time with our friend Jesus in prayer. One of the ways I get to know Jesus better as a friend is to read about him in the Bible. Listen as I read this story. *(Read Luke 2:41-52.)*

"Every year Jesus' parents went to Jerusalem for Passover. And when Jesus was twelve years old, they all went there as usual for the celebration. After Passover his parents left, but they did not know that Jesus had stayed on in the city. They thought he was traveling with some other people, and they went a whole day before they started looking for him. When they could not find him with their relatives and friends, they went back to Jerusalem and started looking for him there.

"Three days later they found Jesus sitting in the temple, listening to the teachers and asking them questions. Everyone who heard him was surprised at how much he knew and at the answers he gave. When his parents found him, they were amazed. His mother said, 'Son, why have you done this to us? Your father and I have been very worried, and we have been searching for you!' Jesus answered, 'Why did you have to look for me? Didn't you know that I would be in my Father's house?' But they did not understand what he meant.

"Jesus went back to Nazareth with his parents and obeyed them. His mother kept on thinking about all that had happened. Jesus became wise, and he grew strong. God was pleased with him and so were the people."

Have any of you ever been lost? Tell us about it. What did it feel like when you realized you were lost? Were you in a dangerous place when you were lost? What was the hardest or scariest part about being lost? *(Allow one or two to share.)*

In this story about Jesus being lost, we find him in a temple. Does it seem strange that a young boy is found inside a temple or church? We usually get lost in a crowd at a shopping mall, or at a baseball game, or at an airport or some other crowded public place.

Although it seems strange to us to be found inside a temple or a church, it wasn't that odd for Jesus, especially since he was around 12 years old. For a 12-year-old boy it was the traditional time for him to go to the temple to begin learning the Jewish law. This fact is probably what led Joseph and Mary to go to the temple looking for Jesus in the first place.

100

Please take the blank piece of paper that I have given you and the couple of crayons. Spread apart so you'll have room to draw. On the paper, briefly sketch what you think the inside of that temple looked like. Don't worry about a lot of details. This is only for background. Good. Now would you add the people in the story? Do you remember who was mentioned in the Gospel? *(Pause, inviting the youngsters to name the teachers, Joseph, Mary, and Jesus.)*

Add the teachers and Jesus' parents, Joseph and Mary, to your picture. But, please, don't draw Jesus yet. Now if you'll put your crayons down, we'll come back to your pictures in a few minutes.

For our prayer today, try to remember the times when you've felt lost. You might have actually been physically lost, or you might have been lost in a different way: perhaps a time when you felt alone or disconnected from your family or friends. In this Gospel, Jesus was lost but was found by his family. Mary and Joseph were responsible for him, but more than that, they cared so much about him. Imagine the relief when they walked in the temple and there he was, safe and happy!

Now we're ready to add the person of Jesus to the picture. Would you draw him in your sketch? *(Pause.)* What do you think his face looked like when he saw his parents? Illustrate these feelings on Jesus' face.

Let's take a few minutes and put ourselves into the picture. But instead of drawing this, let's go there in our imaginations. This is a way you can pray and talk with Jesus. It's important to know that Jesus isn't somewhere far away. Jesus lives within each one of us, in a place deep inside. I call this place the heart room. Your heart room is a place where it's quiet, where you can go anytime you want to and place yourself in the presence of Jesus, your friend. The scene of Jesus in the temple can be our heart room today.

When I pray in the way I'd like to show you, it helps me to close my eyes and tune out any sounds in the background. Let's all close our eyes. Don't worry that you'll be the only one. I'll keep my own eyes open to make sure it's safe for everyone. We close our eyes so we won't be distracted.

I'll lead you now through some helps for praying in our heart room. First, take a deep breath to help you relax. Fine. Let's take another deep breath. We all have our eyes closed. As I lead you through this type of prayer, please use my suggestions to make pictures in your mind.

Picture yourself coming into the temple you just drew. What does it look like? Is it big or small? What is it made of? What sounds do you hear in the temple? Is it decorated beautifully or simply? You see Jesus there. He's a little older than you, so he understands what your feelings are, your likes and dislikes, your dreams and your fears. Jesus has seen you come in and he welcomes you. He motions you to come closer and sit down with him. As you sit next to Jesus, what would you like to say to him? Spend a little time now talking to Jesus. Say whatever you'd like. *(Pause.)* What would Jesus say to you? Listen. *(Pause.)*

(Quietly.) As you end your conversation with Jesus, look at him before we leave this holy temple. Just as when you say goodbye to your friends, tell Jesus whatever you'd like to as you leave the temple. Now say goodbye to Jesus in whatever way you'd like. Wave, hug him, or say some simple words. *(Pause.)* Tell Jesus you'll come back to your heart room again. *(Pause.)* Now imagine yourself walking back to our room here. *(Pause.)*

When you're ready, please open your eyes.

Sometimes it helps to look back on what happened in prayer in our heart rooms.

How did you feel when you were in your heart room? Did you have an easy time talking to Jesus? Do you believe he heard you? Did Jesus say anything to you? Sometimes we hear Jesus and sometimes we don't. That's natural. *(Allow children time to share as they desire.)*

Now that you've had a chance to talk to Jesus in your heart room, you can do this anytime you want. There's no place off-limits for talking to Jesus, no time that's too early or too late. This prayer can be repeated anytime you feel you'd like to talk to Jesus. It's been a good, peaceful place, hasn't it?

Look what I have here. It's baby oil. I'm going to pass some to each of you now and I'd like to invite you to put just a little on your fingers and hold it there. *(Demonstrate. Then wait till each child gets some oil.)*

Go ahead now and rub the oil between your fingers. Do you notice how smooth it feels? Slowly begin to rub the oil into your skin. It has become part of you. The oil has sunk beneath the surface of your skin. This is what God is like. God is always a part of you, beneath your skin. The prayer time today helps remind us of how close God is to all of us during our lives, every day or every night. God loves us just as we are and will never leave us for any reason. We can never be lost from God.

Whenever you rub your hands together, as we just did, that can be a reminder that God loves us as we are and that we will never be lost from God because God is as close as our skin.

Remember what we did here in our retreat. I hope you have many happy and prayerful times with Jesus in your heart room when you pray this way again.

Snack
gingerbread people
milk or juice

Adult-Child Sharing Time

After the adult session, parents or adult retreat leaders join their children in the snack room to begin their sharing time. If weather permits, retreatants can go outside for a nature walk. If not, they might want to find a corner to sit in, take a walk through the church, spread out blankets throughout the room, or even create forts out of blankets to sit in for privacy. We allow approximately twenty minutes for adult-child sharing time, asking all participants to return to the gathering room at the allotted time for our closing.

The questions on p. 214 can facilitate adult-child sharing.

If time remains, parents or adult leaders can help children compose a song to a familiar tune, using the concepts of the retreat.

For example:
(To the tune of "Pop Goes the Weasel")

Whenever we are feeling sad,
Whenever we are angry,
Whenever we are happy or glad,
Let's talk to Jesus.

(To accommodate children who are not auditory learners, print the lyrics of each song on a large poster board and display.)

Closing Prayer

The children can close with song, teaching each other the lyrics their group composed. Following the prayer of joyful song, an adult facilitator leads the children in the following litany:

Adult: I invite all of you to join me in prayer. First, I'll say something to God for all of us. Then you say, "Your love is forever."

Adult:	God our parent, there's nothing we can do or say that will make you go away.
Children:	Your love is forever.
Adult:	God our parent, you love us at least as much as the person who loves us most.
Children:	Your love is forever.
Adult:	God our parent, we will come to you when we're happy or sad.
Children:	Your love is forever.
Adult:	God our parent, we will come to you when we're angry or scared.
Children:	Your love is forever.
Adult:	God our parent, you love us just as we are.
Children:	Your love is forever.

Invite children to join hands and say the Our Father.

Note

1. Dennis Linn, Sheila Fabricant Linn and Matthew Linn, Good Goats: Healing our Image of God (Mahwah, N.J.: Paulist Press, 1994), 11.

7-Respect Retreat

(Luke 19:1-7; Matthew 14:28-31; John 6:1-13)

If giving a family retreat that includes three- to six-year-olds, coordinate with the retreat entitled "Picnic" from *Parent-Child Retreats: Spiritual Experiences for Children Ages 3-6 and Their Parents* (Living the Good News, 1997).

Focus

During Jesus' life on earth, he showed us time and again how to love. For Jesus, love meant respecting, accepting, and honoring people just as they were. He insisted that his followers, too, respect the dignity and uniqueness of each person. Jesus showed us that respect works both ways. He didn't allow people to be unkind to him or to anyone else. When people acted without love, Jesus tried to understand the hurt behind their actions or words. His love often healed their emotional wounds.

Seven- to ten-year-olds sometimes find themselves in a position of being ridiculed, often by other seven-to ten-year-olds. This is a sign, however, of a larger society that ridicules people who are not like themselves. It's imperative that young believers, following Jesus' example, go against this trend. Sadly, children may hear their parents criticize or make fun of people. Without undermining their parents' dignity, we shift the focus to better ways of loving.

This process involves helping children open their eyes to ways they can love within the circumstances of their lives. Giving themselves to others in love might involve sharing their ideas, spreading their happiness, or using their talents to bring people joy. But the best way for children to love is to offer their friendship, even when someone isn't easy to love. With practice, children can become aware that people often behave in unlovable ways when they don't feel good about themselves. Like Jesus' love, children's love can heal.

The focus of the retreat can be summarized in three statements:
▲ Wherever there is love, Jesus is there.
▲ Love means respecting, accepting, and honoring people just as they are.
▲ Yet love does not require us to be treated badly by others.

Preparations Before the Retreat

1. Meet as a team to pray, read, discuss, understand, and interiorize the focus and scriptural basis for the retreat.
2. Discern which team members will be responsible for the gathering presentation, each of the three children's activities, and the adult retreat section, if there is one.
3. If this is to be a family retreat, choose an adult retreat topic from the section entitled Outlines for Parent Sessions (pp. 163-184). If parents will not be present, prepare a letter to send home for parent-child follow-up enrichment (p. 192).
4. Divide the following preparation responsibilities:

Make nametags in three colors.

Collect materials for the environment.
Bible
picture of Jesus
sample souvenir
book for story session

picnic basket

picnic blanket

bulletin board or poster board saying "Wherever there is love, Jesus is there."

Prepare for the gathering presentation.

Write these scrambled phrases on seven large strips of paper:

▲ Wherever there is love

▲ Jesus is there.

▲ Love means

▲ respecting, accepting, and honoring people

▲ just as they are.

▲ Love does not mean

▲ we allow others to treat us badly.

Prepare the retreat souvenir.

First, gather materials.

For each retreatant:

▲ two 2-gallon recloseable plastic bags

▲ the Sit-Upon insert paper (See p. 212.)

For retreatants to share:

▲ masking tape and permanent marker (one for each two students working in a
   group)

▲ several staplers

▲ newspapers cut into strips one inch wide (other stuffing materials such as foam
   pellets or clean pantyhose with runs may be substituted if readily available)

Second, do the advance preparation.

1. Make a sample to determine the amount of stuffing desired for each pillow.

2. Duplicate the Sit-Upon insert (p. 212).

Locate the story.

Obtain *People* by Peter Spier (New York: Doubleday, 1980). If unable to locate
the first choice of literature, substitute *The Rag Coat* by Lauren Mills (Boston:
Little, Brown and Company, 1991) and change letter tp parents.

Prepare for the gathering presentation.

Become familiar with the heart room prayer (p. 114).

Preparation: Cut out enough shapes of round loaves of bread (about the size of
hamburger buns) and fish in the form of the ichthys so that each participant will

receive either a loaf of bread or a fish. (See p. 211.) Provide markers and a large basket.

Purchase groceries and prepare the snack.

▲ bread

▲ peanut butter and jelly *(or other filling)*

▲ lemonade

Duplicate the Adult-Child Sharing Form (p. 214) or letter to parents (p. 192).

Preparations the Day of the Retreat

1. Gather as a team and pray.
2. Set out nametags and safety pins or tape *(warning: no straight pins or strings)*. Have exactly as many nametags as retreatants, and equal numbers of nametags for each color group.
3. Have each retreat team member wear a different colored nametag. This will later help the children divide into groups for their activities.
4. On top of a piano or table, create the environment in the gathering room with an arrangement that reflects the theme of the retreat. Include a picnic blanket, a picnic basket, the book that will be read during the retreat, a sample of the souvenir the children will make, a picture of Jesus, a Bible, and a bulletin board or poster board with the words "Wherever there is love, Jesus is there."
5. Gather all the materials for the retreat souvenir and set out on tables in the room that will be used for this activity.
6. Spread out so that at least one team member is greeting the retreatants as they arrive, one is bringing retreatants (and parents) to the gathering room, one is waiting in the gathering room, and one is directing parents and younger siblings to the nursery.
7. Begin the retreat by warmly greeting the retreatants, then introducing the team members.

Gathering Presentation

Okay, okay. I know what you're thinking. When is she going to tell a joke? Well, you asked the right person: I know a bunch.

Why do blonds—Oh, wait a minute. That one's not very polite.

Uhhh... Oh! Here's one. Your mamma's so old—Oops. That one's not polite either.

Let's see... What's the difference between a Catholic and a—No. That one's not kind.

Hmmmmm... You know what? I've been hearing too many jokes that make fun of people lately. I like to tell only jokes that respect, accept, and honor people as they are, but I can't think of any jokes that do that. Have you noticed that, too?

It's not just jokes, the more I think about it. Raise your hand if you've ever heard someone make fun of someone else. What did that person say?

I think we need to get some advice from Jesus. I'd like to look at his life and see how he had fun without hurting people's feelings. Let's see... *(Thumb through the Bible. Turn to Matthew 14:28-31.)* Oh, listen to this.

"Peter replied, 'Lord, if it is really you, tell me to come to you on the water.' 'Come on!' Jesus said. Peter then got out of the boat and started walking on the water toward him. But when Peter saw how strong the wind was, he was afraid and started sinking. 'Save me, Lord!' he shouted. Right away, Jesus reached out his hand. He helped Peter up and said, 'You surely don't have much faith. Why do you doubt?'"

What would you think if Jesus had said, "You baby, Peter. You scared chicken. Get out of the boat and walk over to me, you baloney brain."

Instead, what did Jesus do? *(Help children repeat Matthew's approximate words: Jesus at once stretched out his hands and caught Peter.)*

That's right. Jesus understood how Peter might be afraid of drowning—many people are. Jesus loved Peter by respecting him, accepting him, and honoring him, even if he was afraid.

Or what about this one? *(Tell the account of Zacchaeus, Luke 19:1-7.)*

"Jesus was going through Jericho, where a man named Zacchaeus lived. He was in charge of collecting taxes and was very rich. Jesus was heading his way, and Zacchaeus wanted to see what he was like. But Zacchaeus was a short man and could not see over the crowd. So he ran ahead and climbed up into a sycamore tree.

"When Jesus got there, he looked up and said, 'Zacchaeus, hurry down! I want to stay with you today.' Zacchaeus hurried down and gladly welcomed Jesus. Everyone who saw this started grumbling, 'This man Zacchaeus is a sinner! And Jesus is going home to eat with him.'"

What if, when Jesus saw Zacchaeus in the tree, he shouted, "Monkey, monkey, in a tree. Shorty, Shorty, hee-hee-hee."

Or what if he said, "What kind of name is Zacchaeus anyway?"

Instead, what did Jesus say to Zacchaeus? *(Help the children repeat Jesus' words: "Zacchaeus, hurry down. I mean to stay at your house today.")*

That's right. Jesus understood that Zacchaeus was probably embarrassed. A lot of us have been embarrassed before, haven't we? But instead of making fun, Jesus loved Zacchaeus by respecting, accepting, and inviting him to come down from the tree and be near him.

Jesus tried hard to understand why his friends acted the way they did, and he accepted them that way.

In fact, if we searched this whole book, the Bible, we would never find a time when Jesus made fun of people. Never.

Sometimes even adults make fun of other people. They must not know that Jesus didn't live his life like that and neither should they. Jesus tried hard to understand why his friends acted the way they did. He did not like what they did, but didn't reject them. He respected, accepted, and honored them just as they were. This is what love is. Whenever people treat us with respect and acceptance, and whenever we treat others the same way, Jesus is there with us. This is the way Jesus lived his life, and so must we.

Even though Jesus never made fun of people and was never mean, he still didn't let people treat him badly.

Think about these incidents. One day people were insulting God by selling things in the temple. Jesus told them they couldn't do that. He told them sternly to get out.

Another time, the devil was daring Jesus to do things he didn't want to do. He said Jesus must not trust God if he wouldn't do these things. Jesus was stern again. He told the devil to leave. He didn't allow the devil to say untrue things about him or ask him to do things he didn't want to do.

We don't have to either. Loving someone never means we have to allow them to treat us badly. Has that ever happened to you? Has anyone ever treated you in a way you didn't like? How did you handle it without being mean? *(Allow several children time to share their experiences. Invite others to suggest ways to handle these situations as Jesus would have. Introduce the problem-solving strategy of "I"*

110

messages: I feel... when you.... Examples: "I feel sad when you call me names." "I feel angry when I hear you telling me I did something I really didn't do." "I feel scared when I hear you yell like that at me.")

(Invite 7 volunteers to hold one of 7 Scrambled Phrases cards containing these words. Challenge them to stand in order so that 3 complete sentences appear. Ask the remaining children to read them out loud and verify that the phrases are in order.)

Scrambled Phrases:

Wherever there is love

Jesus is there.

Love means

respecting, accepting, and honoring people

just as they are.

Love does not mean

we allow others to treat us badly.

We have some fun activities to do now. Let me show you what we'll be doing. *(Show the children the souvenir and story, and tell them they'll also be talking to Jesus.)*

Now look at the color of your nametag. *(Have the children leave the room with the team leader who has the same colored nametag.)*

Children's Activities

The following three children's activities run simultaneously, and the children rotate through them until they've been to all three.

Activity 1: Art as Prayer—Retreat Souvenir

The retreatants will make a Picnic Sit-Upon, which can also be used as a Prayer Pillow when they talk to Jesus in their heart room.

As the children construct a memento of their experience, talk about the focus of the retreat (p.106).

Gather retreatants around the materials table to create a picnic sit-upon/prayer pillow:

1. Participants write their name with permanent marker on one of the plastic bags. *(Supervise carefully as markers can damage clothing.)*
2. Retreat leader reviews the focus of the retreat while distributing the insert papers.

3. Children tear their newspapers into one inch strips. *(Expect it to get noisy and messy for the next 5-7 minutes. Remember the 5,000 at Jesus' picnic. This is joyful noise unto the Lord.)*

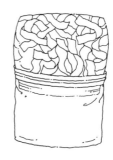

4. Retreatants stuff the filler into one plastic bag. When it is almost full, they release the air, zip the plastic bag, and staple it shut.

5. Children place their full bag upside down inside the second bag, then slip the insert paper between the two layers so it is visible. They then release the air from the second bag, zip it, and staple it for reinforcement.

6. Children, leader, or helper cuts a piece of masking tape the same length as the zipper for each child, and places it sticky side up on the table.

7. Participants place the stapled second bag along the bottom half of the tape and fold the remaining top half of the tape over the sealed portion of the bag, enclosing the sealed portion inside the masking tape. *(Use a second strip of tape if necessary.)*

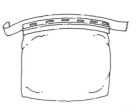

(Children can make pillow cases at home by stitching two bandanas, or pieces of used shower curtains or vinyl tablecloths, together.)

Announce to the children: It's almost time to move to our next prayer session. Please help me get ready for the next group by setting up the table the way it was when you arrived. *(To the final group, give directions about how to put supplies away.)*

Activity 2: Story as Prayer

Story: *People* by Peter Spier (New York: Doubleday, 1980)

As the children listen to and discuss the literature, talk about the focus of the retreat (p. 106).

Greet the children.
(As the children enter the room, designate a space where they can put their belongings, then invite them to sit where they can see the pictures of the book.)

Raise your hand if you've heard this story before. Wonderful. If you have, let's not tell the others what happens so they can enjoy their experience, too.

This is a time of prayer. Let's get ready to listen to what God wants us to hear in this story. Are you in a comfortable position? Let's all take a deep breath and let it out a little at a time.

Introduce the story.

This *non-fiction* book celebrates the uniqueness of people all over the world, their language, appearance, clothing, food, and customs. It encourages acceptance, respect, and honor for everyone.

In this book, Peter Spier, who both wrote and illustrated it, helps us understand that "We all live on the same planet, breathe the same air, and warm ourselves in the same sun." We are all loved by God. In the middle of the book there are two pages that tell about people and their religions. It tells us that there are nine hundred fifty two million Christians in the world. These people believe that Jesus is God like we do. But, there are millions of other people in the world who believe differently. You might already know some of those people. God loves them, too.

Watch for things that people do in our world that are different from the way you do them. Try to learn at least two new facts about some of God's people as we read this story together. At the end we will discuss your findings.

Read the story, taking ample time to show the pictures.

(Using voice intonations, pauses, and a prayerful sense of awe, read the book aloud. Allow time for children to be touched by the words as well as the illustrations. At the conclusion, close the book gently and allow a moment of "think time.")

(Read only the text in large print. Refer to the pictures, pointing out differences. Make no value judgments, keeping comments neutral and allowing God to speak individually to children's hearts. Point out facts from the smaller pictures for children who cannot see the details of these images.)

Talk about the story.

▲ What did you learn about God's people? *(There are many, but no two are alike. God made us all and loves each one of us.)*

▲ What do you think God thinks about people of different religions? *(God made us all and loves each one of us. Like God, we respect and honor people of all religions.)*

▲ How did you feel hearing that some people hate others because they are unlike themselves? *(Reinforce God's view of love and acceptance.)*

▲ Can you remember instances when Jesus spent time with people who were unacceptable to others? How did Jesus treat them? *(Lepers, tax collectors, sinners—Jesus treated them with love and respect.)*

▲ What did you like about this book?

(Hold up the book with the cover facing the children.) When you're telling your family about the book we read during the retreat today, remember this title. Let's say it together: *People.*

Announce to the children: Now it's time to move to the next retreat session. Be sure to take any of your belongings with you on your way out. Let's walk together.

Alternate Story

If the first choice of literature for this session is unavailable, substitute *The Rag Coat* by Lauren Mills (Boston: Little, Brown and Company, 1991).

Introduction:
When Minna wore her newly quilted coat to school, the children laughed at her—until they heard the stories behind each quilt patch. When Minna shares the stories behind the rags in her coat with her classmates, let's see what lesson Minna's classmates learn about respect.

Reading:
(Throughout the story, point out how Minna forgave her classmates for their teasing and invited each of them to touch the part in her new coat that their mothers had made. Even though Minna had been treated badly by them, the love and sharing of their mothers who had made the coat with scraps reminded her that wherever there is love, Jesus is there.)

Discussion:
▲ Tell about something you have that someone made for you. Why is it special to you?

▲ Do you agree with Papa's words, "People only need people, and nothing else?"

▲ Who in this story reminds you of Jesus?

▲ Can you think of a person who gets laughed at or made fun of? Let's share some ideas about how we can love and respect those people.

▲ What was your favorite part of the story? Why?

Activity 3: The Heart Room Prayer

Weave the focus of the retreat throughout the children's experience of the heart room prayer.

114

(Greet the children as they arrive, then invite them to sit in a circle with you. Be sure the circle is large enough that there is room between the children and they don't touch each other.)

You must all have memories of wonderful times you spent with friends and family, right? Today I'd like to tell you about a very famous picnic that took place about 2,000 years ago, and it was so incredible that we're still reading and talking about it today. It might be famous because of all the people who were there. The story says there were over 5,000 people. That wonderful picnic could also be famous because of the food. The menu wasn't what we usually think of as picnic food. If I were to ask you what you would plan on bringing to a picnic, what food would you suggest? *(Encourage responses.)* It's interesting to compare your menu with what was served at this large, famous picnic. The only food that day was bread and fish!

I would like to read you the story of this famous event. It's in Matthew's gospel, and also in Mark's and Luke's gospels. That's how important the story of this picnic is. But today we're going to read from John's gospel (John 6:1-13). As I read this story, would you listen for anything in the story that you think is unusual or dramatic? *(Read the gospel slowly and thoughtfully, pausing often, particularly after verse 9.)*

"Jesus crossed Lake Galilee, which was also known as Lake Tiberias. A large crowd had seen him work miracles to heal the sick, and those people went with him. It was almost time for the Jewish festival of Passover, and Jesus went up on a mountain with his disciples and sat down.

"When Jesus saw the large crowd coming toward him, he asked Philip, 'Where will we get enough food to feed all these people?' He said this to test Philip, since he already knew what he was going to do.

"Philip answered, 'Don't you know that it would take almost a year's wages just to buy only a little bread for each of these people?'

"Andrew, the brother of Simon Peter, was one of the disciples. He spoke up and said, 'There is a boy here who has five small loaves of barley bread and two fish.' (Pause.) 'But what good is that with all these people?'

"The ground was covered with grass and Jesus told his disciples to have everyone sit down. About five thousand men were in the crowd. Jesus took the bread in his hands and gave thanks to God. Then he passed the bread to the people, and he did the same with the fish, until everyone had plenty to eat.

"The people ate all they wanted, and Jesus told his disciples to gather up the left-overs, so that nothing would be wasted. The disciples gathered them up and filled twelve large baskets with what was left over from the five barley loaves."

What struck you as unusual or dramatic in this story? *(Affirm all observations.)* The gospel has many interesting things in it, as you pointed out. But one line in particular, verse 9, about the young boy sharing his lunch with all those people, is something that makes this story significant for us.

Do you remember what kind of bread the boy had? John writes that he had five barley loaves. I would like you to picture the barley loaf. Make a circle with your two hands about the size of a hamburger bun. That's about the size of the boy's loaves of bread. In those days a loaf of bread was smaller and shaped differently than our loaves of bread today. His five tiny loaves seemed hardly enough to feed 5,000! That's important, because in those days barley was the only kind of bread that the poor people could afford. So we know that the little boy who shared his food that day was poor.

After hearing this story, what do you think was the miracle that happened here at the picnic? *(Allow 1 or 2 to respond.)* Yes, multiplying those few loaves for over 5,000 people was quite a feat, you're right. But the real miracle of that day was that a young boy was willing to share the food that he had brought for his lunch. In order for Jesus to feed all those people, he had to depend on that child. Without his willingness to share, we're not sure what would have happened at the picnic that day.

(Give each child a marker and paper shaped as either a loaf of bread or a fish.)

I'm giving each of you either a loaf of bread or a fish. Notice the way the fish looks. There's an interesting story about this type of fish, which we call an ichthys. Can you say that with me? Ichthys. After Jesus' death, followers of Jesus were often punished, so they were afraid to tell anyone they were friends of Jesus. Instead, they used the fish-shaped symbol to let each other know they were Christians. The word *ichthys* is a Greek word, and it means "fish." But the letters i-c-h-t-h-y-s are also the first letters of the Greek words that mean, "Jesus Christ, Son of God, Savior." Let's think of that story when we use our fish today.

Since we are friends of Jesus, too, Jesus would like us to give something of ourselves to other people. We don't have to share our lunch all the time. Instead, we can share something about ourselves that would make another person's life better. We can share our ideas, our good moods, or, most importantly, our friendship. We can also share our talents. As I read this important line in the gospel, would you think of the specific talent that you are able to share with others? If you think of more than one, that's great.

Now listen. "There is a boy here... there is a girl here... who has five barley loaves and two fish, but what good are these for so many?" Rather than barley loaves and fish, what talents are you willing to share with other people? Is your talent being a kind listener? Being a good friend? Do you sing well? Are you funny? Good at teaching other kids to play sports? Do you read well? Draw well? Think of a talent you have that you can share with other people. Right now, write or draw a picture on your loaf or fish of something you're good at that you are willing to share with other people. *(Allow time for children to write or draw. Be available to help youngsters articulate their talents. The adult leader should include a talent also. Ask a child to collect the loaves and fish in the basket.)*

I'm going to shake up this basket and as I come around, please take one shape. If you had a fish to write or draw on before, choose a loaf this time. If you had a loaf, choose a fish. *(After each child has a shape, the adult leader should choose one as well. Ask a volunteer to re-read John 6:9-11.)* Remember when John wrote that the child was willing to share his food? Then he asked, "But what good is that with all these people?" Let's use our own suggestions of talents we can share in a litany. A litany is a list of short prayers. After I say each prayer, everyone answers that they agree with the prayer. As we read each talent, please answer: "This is good for many people." Let's practice what we'll say after each person reads their talent in our litany. "This is good for many people."

(After leading the litany, thank the children for their suggestions. Challenge them to find ways they can share their talents in the coming week. They may also want to use a suggestion they heard from someone else during the week.)

Who would like to read what Jesus did after the people all had their fill of the picnic lunch? *(Have the volunteer re-read v.11-13.)* Jesus collected the food so it would not be wasted. Now we also collect our talents. We use our talents so they're not wasted. *(Ask the retreatants to place their shapes into the basket as it is passed.)*

I'd like to show you a way you can pray and talk with Jesus now. It's important to know, though, that Jesus isn't somewhere far away. Jesus lives within each one of us, in a place deep inside. I call this place the heart room. Your heart room is a place where it's quiet, where you can go anytime you want to and place yourself in the presence of Jesus, your friend.

It helps me to close my eyes and tune out any sounds. Let's all close our eyes. Don't worry that you'll be the only one. I'll keep my own eyes open to make sure it's safe for everyone. All of us have our eyes closed so we won't be distracted.

I'll lead you now through some helps for praying this way. First, take a deep breath to help you relax. Fine. Let's take another deep breath. We all have our eyes closed. As I lead you through this type of prayer please use my suggestions to make pictures in your mind.

Let's imagine ourselves at a large picnic. Imagine what the picnic spot looks like. Is it a park? A lake? A meadow? *(Pause.)* Feel the sun on your skin. *(Pause.)* Smell the hamburgers cooking. *(Pause.)* Listen to the rustling of the leaves of that large tree. *(Pause.)* Someone walks over to you. It's Jesus. *(Pause.)* What does he look like? What color is his hair? Is it curly? Straight? Long? Short? *(Pause.)* Now look at his face. Is he smiling? How does he look at you? *(Pause.)* When you look at his face do you feel peaceful, happy? What are your feelings when you look at Jesus' face? How is Jesus dressed? What color is his skin?

Jesus sits down next to you. He wants to spend time with you alone. *(Pause.)* Make yourself comfortable next to Jesus. He's there only for you. Jesus tells you what a special child you are. He explains that God made you with wonderful talents that you can share to help other people. Listen to Jesus as he talks to you. *(Wait 30 seconds.)* What would you like to say to Jesus? In our heart room, we don't have to worry that we might say the wrong thing or that Jesus might not understand us. Knowing we're with such an incredibly good friend, let's take a minute to talk with Jesus right now. I'll stop for a short time and you can tell Jesus whatever you would like. *(Wait 30 seconds.)*

It's time to go now. Say goodbye to Jesus in whatever way you'd like. Wave, hug him, or say some simple words. *(Pause.)* Tell Jesus you'll come back to your heart room again. *(Pause.)* Now imagine yourself walking back to our room here. *(Pause.)*

When you're ready, please open your eyes.

Sometimes it helps to look back on what happened in prayer in our heart rooms.

How did you feel when you were in your heart room? Did you have an easy time talking to Jesus? Do you believe he heard you? Did Jesus say anything to you? Sometimes we hear Jesus and sometimes we don't. That's natural. *(Allow children time to share.)*

Now that you've had a chance to talk to Jesus in your heart room, you can do this anytime you want. There's no place off-limits for talking to Jesus, no time that's too early or too late. This prayer can be repeated anytime you'd like to talk to Jesus. It's been a good, peaceful place, hasn't it?

Remember what we did here in our retreat. I hope you have many happy and prayerful times with Jesus in your heart room whenever you decide to pray this way again.

Snack

peanut butter and jelly sandwiches
lemonade

Adult-Child Sharing Time

After the adult session, parents or adult retreat leaders join their children in the snack room to begin their sharing time. If weather permits, retreatants can go outside for a nature walk. If not, they might want to find a corner to sit in, take a walk through the church, spread out blankets throughout the room, or even create forts out of blankets to sit in for privacy. We allow approximately twenty minutes for adult-child sharing time, asking all participants to return to the gathering room at the allotted time for our closing.

The questions on p. 214 can facilitate adult-child sharing.

If time remains, parents or adult leaders can help children compose a song to a familiar tune, using the concepts of the retreat.

For example:
(To the tune of "This Land is Your Land")

> Is your talent kindness?
> Could it be listening?
> Is your talent joking?
> How is your teaching?
> Is your talent drawing?
> How 'bout respecting?
> Aren't ya glad we're not alike?

(To accommodate children who are not auditory learners, print the lyrics of each song on a large poster board and display.)

Closing Prayer

The children can close with song, teaching each other the lyrics their group composed. Following the prayer of joyful song, an adult facilitator leads the children in the following litany:

Adult: I invite all of you to join me in prayer. First, I'll say something to God for all of us. Then you say, "God is love."

Adult: Loving God, wherever there is love, you are there.

Children: God is love.

Adult: Loving God, just as you love us, we love one another.

Children: God is love.

Adult: Loving God, love means respecting, accepting, and honoring people just as they are.

Children: God is love.

Adult: Loving God, when people are unkind to us, we will solve the problem peacefully.

Children: God is love.

Adult: Loving God, we will always act in kindness.

Children: God is love.

Invite children to join hands and say the Our Father.

8-Shining Light Retreat

(Luke 11:33-36)

If giving a family retreat that includes three- to six-year-olds, coordinate with the retreat entitled "Candle" from *Parent-Child Retreats: Spiritual Experiences for Children Ages 3-6 and Their Parents* (Living the Good News, 1997).

Focus

The spiritual gift of goodness can confuse children because of the ways they've heard the term used. "Be good" has been a nebulous guideline for living, covering everything from "Stop complaining" to "Don't talk in class" to "Behave-like-I-wish-you-would." Yet goodness is a fruit of the life centered in God, given us by the indwelling of Jesus' spirit.

Central to this retreat is the theology of the indwelling Spirit. Our goodness is the glory God gives us by manifesting Jesus in us. If we allow it, Jesus will shine forth. For children, their friendship with Jesus is the source of their goodness. When they display the qualities of Jesus, the fruits of the Holy Spirit, they light up the lives of people around them.

The indwelling God continues to transform us, and we reassure children that God understands and loves all parts of us—the mischievous as well as the proper, the unpolished as well as the glowing, the shadow as well as the light. But life offers us opportunities to behave as Jesus would, to choose the loving course of action. For children to grow in awareness of this light within them is a significant step in the spiritual journey.

The focus of the retreat can be summarized in three statements:
▲ God dwells within us.
▲ Because of this, people can see Jesus if we allow Jesus to shine forth.
▲ We're good because of our friendship with Jesus. Being good means people feel good when they're with us because we're so much like Jesus.

Preparations Before the Retreat

1. Meet as a team to pray, read, discuss, understand, and interiorize the focus and scriptural basis for the retreat.
2. Discern which team members will be responsible for the gathering presentation, each of the three children's activities, and the adult retreat section, if there is one.
3. If this is to be a family retreat, choose an adult retreat topic from the section entitled Outlines for Parent Sessions (p. 163-184). If parents will not be present, prepare a letter to send home for parent-child follow-up enrichment (p. 193).
4. Divide preparation responsibilities. Use the gifts of the community to lighten the load. Parents, teenagers, school children, and senior citizens can all help prepare.

Make nametags in three colors.

Collect materials for the environment.

Bible

picture of Jesus

sample souvenir

book for story session

a flashlight or camping lantern

a candle

bulletin board or poster board with the words "Jesus shines through us."

optional: a jack-o-lantern with a lighted candle inside

Prepare the retreat souvenir (p. 127).

First, gather materials.

For each retreatant:

▲ Cardboard tube (bathroom tissue size)

▲ four-inch square wax paper

▲ thick rubber band

▲ scissors

▲ file folder label

For retreatants to share:

▲ glue (one for every two retreatants)

▲ Sunday comics section of the newspaper, giftwrap, or colored paper

▲ two or three metal or plastic kazoos for demonstration

Second, do the advance preparation.

1. Cut the wax paper for the number of retreatants registered.

2. Cut the comics, wrapping paper, or brightly colored paper (not as heavy as construction paper) the length of the tubes and longer than the circumference to overlap by one inch.

3. Make a sample kazoo to use at the retreat.

Locate the story.

Obtain *The Boy Who Held Back the Sea* by Thomas Locker (New York: Dial Books, 1987). If unable to locate the first literature choice, substitute *The Treasure* by Uri Shulevitz (Canada: Harper Collins, 1986) and change parent's letter.

Prepare for the gathering presentation.

Prepare 10-12 strips of poster board with magnetic strips on the back. On seven of them, write the following descriptors. Leave the rest blank. If preferred, use overhead transparencies to display the words.

We say loving things to each other.
We are full of goodness.
We are kind.
People feel good when they're with us.
We complain constantly when we're unhappy.
We're crabby to our family.
We don't care about what other people want.

Become familiar with the heart room prayer (p. 130).

Gather materials: large sheet of paper, marker, markers or pencils for each child, flashlight, blindfold, one small brown paper bag for each participant; 3 small balls of different colors, 3 pencils of different colors, and 3 small sheets of paper of different colors

Purchase groceries and prepare the snack.

▲ bananas

▲ pretzels

▲ milk or orange juice

Duplicate the Adult-Child Sharing Form (p. 214) or letter to parents (p. 193).

Preparations the Day of the Retreat

1. Gather as a team and pray.
2. Set out nametags and safety pins or tape *(warning: no straight pins or strings)*. Have exactly as many nametags as retreatants, and equal numbers of nametags for each color group.
3. Have each retreat team member wear a different colored nametag. This will later help the children divide into groups for their activities.
4. On top of a piano or table, create the environment in the gathering room with an arrangement that reflects the theme of the retreat. Include the book that will be read during the retreat, a sample of the souvenir the children will make, and a Bible, a picture of Jesus, a flashlight, or camping lantern, a candle, and a bulletin board or poster with the words "Jesus shines through us." If this retreat is near Halloween, include a jack-o-lantern with a lighted candle inside.
5. Gather all the materials for the retreat souvenir and set out on tables in the room that will be used for this activity.
6. Spread out so that at least one team member is greeting the retreatants as they arrive, one is bringing retreatants (and parents) to the gathering room, one is

waiting in the gathering room, and one is directing parents and younger siblings to the nursery.

7. Begin the retreat by warmly greeting the retreatants, then introducing the team members.

Gathering Presentation

(This game is called Concept Attainment, a process of induction. By discerning what the "yes" responses have in common, children are interacting with the attributes of that concept before they determine the concept itself. In this retreat the concept they'll "attain" is "Being Like Jesus." Allow at least 10 minutes. Write each descriptor on an overhead or place magnetic strips bearing the descriptors on the chalkboard.)

I'm thinking of something that has to do with Jesus. I'm going to write words under the word "Yes" or "No." If I write the word or words under "Yes," it means those words describe the idea I want you to guess. If I write the words under "No," it means the words do *not* describe the idea I want you to guess.

Remember, the idea *has to do with* Jesus, but "Jesus" is not the idea I want you to guess. Let's start.

We say loving things to each other. This is a "Yes." Now stop and think about what saying kind things to each other might describe. Think about what saying kind things to each other has to do with Jesus, but don't say anything out loud.

Let's go on.

When we're unhappy, we make everyone's life miserable by complaining constantly. This is a "No." Stop and think about why making everyone's life miserable by constantly complaining *does not* describe an idea that has to do with Jesus. Now think about it, but don't say anything out loud.

We say loving things to each other. Let's all say, "Yes!"

We complain constantly when we're unhappy. Let's all say, "No!"

Let's keep going. Remember, if the word or words are a "Yes," it means those words describe the idea I want you to guess.

Here's another "Yes." *We are full of goodness.* Think about why "We are full of goodness" has something to do with Jesus. What does Jesus have to do with the fact that *we* are full of goodness?

Here's another "Yes." *We are kind.* Hmmmm. What do "We are kind," "We are full of goodness," and "We say loving things to each other," all have in common? What do they describe? Remember, just think. Don't say anything out loud.

We're crabby to our family. This is a... "No." That's right. I think you're starting to discover the idea.

Where should this one go? *People feel good when they're with us.* That's right. It's a "Yes."

Let's look at all these "Yesses."

We say kind things to each other.

We are full of goodness.

We are kind.

People feel good when they're with us.

Hmmmm. I wonder what all these things describe.

Let's look at the "No's."

We complain constantly when we're unhappy.

We're crabby to our family.

Where might we put this description—under "Yes" or under "No"?

We don't care about what other people want.

That's right, it's a "No."

Now let's stop and think again.

We're thinking of something that has to do with Jesus. The word or words under "Yes" mean those words describe the idea I want you to guess. The words under "No" mean the words do *not* describe the idea I want you to guess.

Remember, the idea *has to do with* Jesus, but "Jesus" is not the idea I want you to guess. What could that important idea be?

Gabriela, you look like you might have an idea. Don't tell us, but if you think you know, tell us something that would be a "Yes." *(Accept any answer that describes what it's like to be like Jesus. If the child suggests something that doesn't fit the concept of "Being like Jesus," put the answer in the "No" column. Thank her for the suggestion, pointing out that it's a "No.")*

Sam, you really want to tell us what the idea is. First, though, can you give us an example of a "No?" *(Accept any answer that does not describe being like Jesus.)*

(Spend a bit more time suggesting or receiving suggestions for "Yes" and "No" descriptors, adding to each list.)

Who knows what idea we're trying to think of that has to do with Jesus?

(Accept any answer that sufficiently equates to "Being like Jesus." Possible answers: "We are (or act) like Jesus"; "Jesus loves us and we love each other"; "Everything we say about ourselves is true about Jesus, too." Write the concept "Being like Jesus" at the top of the list.)

You're such good guessers! We learned a lot about being like Jesus by playing this game.

Jesus lives inside each one of us. He's like a candle inside us, and because of that, warmth and light, kindness and goodness shine forth from us. People can feel the goodness, kindness, and warmth of Jesus whenever they spend time with us. We're full of goodness simply because we're friends with Jesus. Our goodness is as bright as a candle flickering in the dark. People are thankful for our goodness because it means that when they're with us, they feel loved. They feel loved by us and they feel loved by Jesus. That's what it means to be like Jesus.

We have some fun activities to do now. Let me show you what we'll be doing. *(Show the children the souvenir and story, and tell them they'll also be talking to Jesus.)*

Children's Activities

The following three children's activities run simultaneously, and the children rotate through them until they've been to all three.

Activity 1: Art as Prayer— Retreat Souvenir

The retreatants will make a Cardboard Tube Kazoo.

To introduce the retreat souvenir, the adult leader hums into a plastic or metal kazoo a church tune familiar to the children, such as "This Little Light of Mine." Point out that sharing music with each other in friendship is one way of letting the joy of Jesus shine forth.

As the children construct their kazoos, talk about the focus of the retreat (p. 122).

Gather retreatants around the materials table to create their cardboard kazoos.

1. Children glue decorative paper to cover the tube.
2. They place wax paper over one end of the tube, wrap it tightly against the tube, and secure it with a rubber band.
3. With the scissors, retreatants cut a 1/4" hole into the cardboard near the wax paper end of the tube. They can create a tune by placing the open end of the kazoo to their mouths and humming the sound "doo-doo-doo."
4. Children write their names on their kazoos.
5. As participants finish their kazoos, they can practice creating music in small groups. If time remains, retreatants can perform for each other.

Activity 2: Story as Prayer

Story: *The Boy Who Held Back the Sea* by Thomas Locker (New York: Dial Books, 1987)

As the children listen to and discuss the literature, talk about the focus of the retreat (p. 122).

Greet the children.
(As retreatants enter the room, designate a space where they can put their belongings, then invite them to sit where they can see the pictures of the book.)

Raise your hand if you've heard this story before. Wonderful. if you have, let's not tell the others what happens so they can enjoy their experience, too.

This is a time of prayer. Let's get ready to listen to what God wants to hear in this story. Are you in a comfortable position? Let's all take a deep breath and let it out a little at a time.

Introduce the story.
Adapted from *Hans Brinker: or, The Silver Skates,* this tale of Holland spotlights a boy named Jan who single-handedly saved everybody in his town from "the worst flood since Noah."

Jan, the boy in this book, wasn't thought of as a hero around his town. In fact, he was a boy who could sometimes be found watching the sea instead of studying. He even did a few naughty things along the way. Listen for them. If we were looking for someone in this story that reminded us of Jesus, it might not be Jan. But Jan changed. Just as Jan could see light shine through the dike, we start to see the light inside Jan begin to shine. He wanted to do the right thing.

Read the story, taking ample time to show the pictures.

(Using voice intonations, pauses, and a prayerful sense of awe, read the book aloud. Allow time for children to be touched by the words as well as the illustrations. The illustrations are especially important in this book. Help the children notice the darkness in most of the illustrations, and point out when it starts to brighten. At the conclusion, close the book gently and allow a moment of "think time.")

Talk about the story.

▲ What was some of that mischief Jan did? *(He shot a rock through the school window, threw a chunk of pie onto a statue, and ate the pie intended for the miller.)*

▲ When the dike leaked, what were some of the solutions he tried? *(Dirt, a wadded handkerchief, then finally his finger wrapped in the handkerchief.)*

▲ At what point in the story did Jan start acting like you think Jesus might have?

▲ Did he do anything else that Jesus might have done? *(He didn't stay for the festival. He spent time with the blind man.)*

▲ And what about Pieter and his grandmother—was either of them like Jesus? *(The grandmother told a parable for Pieter to learn from.)*

(Hold up the book with the cover facing the children.) When you're telling your family about the book you read during your retreat today, remember this title. Let's say it together: *The Boy Who Held Back the Sea.*

Announce to the children: Now it's time to move to your next retreat session. Be sure to take any of your belongings with you on your way out. Let's walk together.

Alternate Story

If the first choice of literature for this retreat session is unavailable, use *The Treasure* by Uri Shulevitz (Canada: Harper Collins, 1986).

Introduction:
This Caldecott Honor book tells of a poor man who traveled to a faraway city looking for a treasure, only to be told to return home to find it. He finally found the treasure under his own stove at home. Isaac built a house of prayer with the words, "Sometimes one must travel far to discover what is near," which he posted for all to see. He sent the Captain a ruby as a thank-you gift and was never poor again.

Reading:
(Throughout the story, emphasize how far the man traveled to find what had always been close by.)

Discussion:
▲ What was the treasure in this story?

▲ What treasure do we have within us? *(Jesus.)*

▲ How did Isaac share his treasure? *(He gave a ruby to the Captain and posted a sign as his prayer.)*

▲ How can we share our treasure? *(We can let Jesus shine forth in us.)*

▲ If you could build a house of prayer, what would it be like? Where would it be?

▲ Who in the story was like Jesus?

Activity 3: The Heart Room Prayer

Weave the focus of the retreat throughout the children's experience of the heart room prayer.

(Greet the children as they arrive, then invite them to sit in a circle with you. Be sure the circle is large enough that there is room between the children and they don't touch each other. Welcome the children.)

Have you ever thought about light? We have it all around us, but I bet you usually don't think much about it. I know I don't—unless the electricity goes out and there is no light!

Can you add anything to my list of things that would happen if we had no light? Here's what I thought of: We couldn't see the world. Flowers wouldn't grow. And we wouldn't know what our friends looked like. What would you add to my list?

Today we read a short story that Luke wrote where Jesus tells his followers something about light. *(Read Luke 11:33-36.)*

"No one lights a lamp and then hides it or puts it under a clay pot. A lamp is put on a lampstand, so that everyone who comes into the house can see the light. Your eyes are the lamp for your body. When your eyes are good, you have all the light you need. But when your eyes are bad, everything is dark. So be sure that your light isn't darkness. If you have light, and nothing is dark, then light will be everywhere, as when a lamp shines brightly on you."

Luke wrote that our eyes allow the light to enter our body. If our eyes are not healthy, we're not able to see light. Who would like to volunteer to wear this blindfold for an experiment? *(Put the blindfold on the volunteer. Hold three of the same objects—balls, pencils, or paper—before the child.)*

By feeling, what do you think this object is? Will you hand me the red one? Now hand me the yellow one. And now the blue one. *(Remove the blindfold.)*

(Elicit feelings from the "blind" volunteer as he/she was asked to hand over a certain color of object. Ask the spectators how they felt when someone who couldn't see had to perform such an impossible task.)

(If time allows, ask for a second and third volunteer and repeat the task, this time using a different object of three different colors. Ask the child to guess what the object is and to choose a specific color. Then ask him or her to describe how it felt to try to choose without being able to see.)

Jesus tells us that when our body is full of light and no part of it is in darkness, then we will be like a lamp, shining for other people. Listen as I reread Luke's story. *(Read.)*

Can you think of three ways you can shed light into other people's lives by the way you live? What are some ways we can be loving and kind? *(Ask for suggestions. As the children share, write and draw a sketch of their suggestions where all can see.)*

(Give each child a paper bag and marker.) On our brown paper bags, let's all write or draw three ways we can be like light to other people by being loving and kind. You can copy three from our list, or come up with your own. *(Give the children time to make their lists.)*

I'm going to make the room dark now, but I'll turn on this flashlight so we can still see. Now I'm going to let each one of you use the flashlight. When you get it, place it inside your bag, gathering the sack around the bottom to keep the light in the bag, like this. *(Demonstrate.)* Show us your bag, and then tell us *one* of the three ways you choose to let Jesus' light shine through you to the people you know and meet. I'll start.

(After each child has had a turn, take the flashlight and place it into a bag, gathering the sack around the handle of the flashlight. Reread the passage from Luke for a final time. Turn on the lights and debrief with the children. Explain that it is important to listen to each other and respect what another says. Urge them to contribute freely and willingly their reactions. Ask open-ended questions, such as, "What did you learn about Jesus during that prayer time?")

Now I'd like to show you a way you can pray and talk with Jesus. It's important to know, though, that Jesus isn't somewhere far away. Jesus lives within each one of us, in a place deep inside. I call this place the heart room. Your heart room is a place where it's quiet, where you can go anytime you want to and place yourself in the presence of Jesus, your friend.

It helps me to close my eyes and tune out any sounds. Let's all close our eyes. Don't worry that you'll be the only one. I'll keep my own eyes open to make sure it's safe for everyone. All of us have our eyes closed so we won't be distracted.

I'll lead you now through some helps for praying in our heart room. First, take a deep breath to help you relax. Fine. Let's take another deep breath. We all have our eyes closed. As I lead you through this type of prayer, please use my suggestions to make pictures in your mind.

You're sitting in a place deep within yourself. It's a quiet place, a place you love to be. Imagine what this place looks like in your mind. *(Pause.)* There's a candle in front of you in this place called the heart room. Watch the candle flicker and light up your heart room. *(Pause.)* Someone just walked into the room, your heart room. It's Jesus. *(Pause.)* What does he look like? What color is his hair? Is it curly? Straight? Long? Short? *(Pause.)* Now look at his face. Is he smiling? How does he look at you? *(Pause.)* When you look at his face do you feel peaceful, happy? What are your feelings when you look at Jesus' face? How is Jesus dressed? What color is his skin?

Jesus sits down next to you. *(Pause.)* Make yourself comfortable next to Jesus. He's there only for you. What would you like to say to Jesus? In our heart room, we don't have to worry that we might say the wrong thing or that Jesus might not understand us. Knowing we're with such an incredibly good friend, let's take a minute to talk with Jesus right now. I'll stop for a short time and you can tell Jesus whatever you would like. Jesus might also want to say something to you. So listen...

(Wait 60 seconds.)

It's time to go now. Say goodbye to Jesus in whatever way you'd like. Wave, hug him, or say some simple words. *(Pause.)* Tell Jesus you'll come back to your heart room again. *(Pause.)* Now imagine yourself walking back to our room here. *(Pause.)*

When you're ready, please open your eyes.

Sometimes it helps to look back on what happened in prayer in our heart rooms.

How did you feel when you were in your heart room? Did you have an easy time talking to Jesus? Do you believe he heard you? Did Jesus say anything to you? Sometimes we hear Jesus and sometimes we don't. That's natural. *(Allow children time to share.)*

Now that you've had a chance to talk to Jesus in your heart room, you can do this anytime you want. There's no place off-limits for talking to Jesus, no time that's too early or too late. This prayer can be repeated anytime you feel you'd like to talk to Jesus. It's been a good, peaceful place, hasn't it?

Remember what we did here in our retreat. I hope you have many happy and prayerful times with Jesus in your heart room when you pray this way again.

(Invite the children to take their paper bags home as a reminder of this retreat and their possibility of being a light to others in their lives.)

Snack

banana-pretzel candles *(a peeled banana half topped with a stick pretzel for a wick)*

milk or orange juice

Adult-Child Sharing Time

After the adult session, parents or adult retreat leaders join their children in the snack room to begin their sharing time. If weather permits, retreatants can go outside for a nature walk. If not, they might want to find a corner to sit in, take a walk through the church, spread out blankets throughout the room, or even create forts out of blankets to sit in for privacy. We allow approximately twenty minutes for adult-child sharing time, asking all participants to return to the gathering room at the allotted time for our closing.

The questions on p. 214 can facilitate adult-child sharing.

If time remains, parents or adult leaders can help children compose a song to a familiar tune, using the concepts of the retreat.

For example:
(To the tune of "Hokey Pokey")

> I let my light shine out,
> I let my smile beam bright,
> I let my feelings show

So-o other people know.

The light that they can see

Is Jesus' light inside of me.

Easy as 1-2-3.

(To accommodate children who are not auditory learners, print the lyrics of each song on a large poster board and display.)

Closing Prayer

The children can close with song, teaching each other the lyrics their group composed. Following the prayer of joyful song, an adult facilitator leads the children in the following litany:

Adult:	I invite all of you to join me in prayer. First, I'll say something to God for all of us. Then you say, "You dwell within us."
Adult:	God who loves us, we welcome you into our lives.
Children:	You dwell within us.
Adult:	God who loves us, people can see Jesus in us.
Children:	You dwell within us.
Adult:	God who loves us, we're good because of our friendship with Jesus.
Children:	You dwell within us.
Adult:	God who loves us, because of our goodness, people feel good when they're with us.
Children:	You dwell within us.
Adult:	God who loves us, we promise to let Jesus shine through us.
Children:	You dwell within us.

Invite children to join hands and say the Our Father.

9-Presence Retreat

(Luke 1:26; Luke 2:8-20)

If giving a family retreat that includes three- to six-year-olds, coordinate with the retreat entitled "Christmas" from *Parent-Child Retreats: Spiritual Experiences for Children Ages 3-6 and Their Parents* (Living the Good News, 1997).

Focus

Jesus' Incarnation is deeply meaningful to believers. With his birth, the world came to know a new way of living: God with us in Jesus. Love and kindness were Jesus' hallmarks, and the language of love remains today the most significant sign of Christ's presence in us. When we extend ourselves to others in love, we are messengers of God's love to them.

Because Jesus once lived an ordinary earthly life, like us in every way but sin, he can speak most profoundly to children today in the ordinary events of life.

Seemingly insignificant life events—a caring telephone call, the antics of a family pet, or an act of kindness—can signal to children that Jesus wants to be a part of their lives. We help the young retreatants open their eyes to these daily revelations and, in so doing, grow in faith.

Jesus also speaks to us in the stillness of our hearts. Already sensitive to their intuitions, children, with our guidance, learn to trust this gift more and to listen to God speaking within. But children's lives are active, and sometimes overly structured, which, when exaggerated, causes a barrier to hearing the quiet stirrings of God within. Christmas—that time when we await Christ's Incarnation—is an opportunity to enter into stillness and tune into the presence of God in the ordinary.

The focus of the retreat can be summarized in four statements:
▲ The word Incarnation means that God's son became human like us.
▲ As a person living among us, Jesus was a messenger of God's love, as we are.
▲ Jesus is still present to us, in the ordinary things of life.
▲ Stillness helps us be close to Jesus because it allows us time to notice Jesus and to listen to what Jesus might want to say to us.

Preparations Before the Retreat

1. Meet as a team to pray, read, discuss, understand, and interiorize the focus and scriptural basis for the retreat.
2. Discern which team members will be responsible for the gathering presentation, each of the three children's activities, and the adult retreat section, if there is one.
3. If this is to be a family retreat, choose an adult retreat topic from the section entitled Outlines for Parent Sessions (p. 163-184). If parents will not be present, prepare a letter to send home for parent-child follow-up enrichment (p. 194).
4. Divide preparation responsibilities:

Make nametags in three colors.

Collect materials for the environment.
Bible
picture of Jesus

136   *Parent-Child Retreats* sample souvenir

book for story session

a large rock

angel figurines

nativity scene

bulletin board or poster board saying "Jesus is present to us in ordinary things."

Prepare the retreat souvenir (p. 142).

First, gather materials one per retreatant:

▲ 8 1/2" x 11" stiff white paper

▲ 10" x 13" piece heavy duty aluminum foil

▲ 48 inch piece string

▲ scissors

▲ pencil

For retreatants to share:

▲ masking tape

▲ white school glue (one for every two retreatants—not paste)

▲ watercolor paints (one box for each two retreatants), small brushes, and small dishes of water

▲ selection of crayons/markers/colored pencils

▲ tape recorder and soft instrumental music

Second, do the advance preparation.

1. Gently fold each aluminum foil piece in half, touching the top to the bottom to form a 6 1/2" x 10" piece.

2. To form a frame, cut out a 4" square piece from the middle. Start at the fold, 3 inches from the side, and cut up 2 inches. Cut across to the right 4 inches, then down 2 inches returning to the fold.

3. Gently reopen the foil. Cut in diagonally 1 1/2 inches beginning at each inside corner going toward the outside corner. Keep these as flat as possible for retreatants. Make a sample for showing at the retreat.

Locate the story.

Obtain *Sylvester and the Magic Pebble* by William Steig (New York: Simon & Schuster Inc., 1969). If unable to locate the first literature choice, substitute *Wilfrid Gordon McDonald Partridge* by Mem Fox (Brooklyn, N.Y.: Kane/Miller, 1985).

Prepare for the gathering presentation.

Become familiar with the heart room prayer (p. 146).

Gather materials.

▲ a variety of pictures of angels

▲ a telephone, an answering machine, and a beeper *(If any of these is impossible to bring, delete it from the script.)*

▲ clear or masking tape

▲ a blackboard and chalk or newsprint and markers

Purchase groceries and prepare the snack.

▲ angel-shaped cookies

▲ milk

Duplicate the Adult-Child Sharing Form (p. 214) or letter to parents (p. 194).

Preparations the Day of the Retreat

1. Gather as a team and pray.
2. Set out nametags and safety pins or tape *(warning: no straight pins or string.)* Have exactly as many nametags as retreatants, and equal numbers of nametags for each color group.
3. Have each retreat team member wear a different colored nametag. This will later help the children divide into groups for their activities.
4. On top of a piano or table, create the environment in the gathering room with an arrangement that reflects the theme of the retreat. Include the book that will be read during the retreat, a sample of the souvenir the children will make, a Bible, a large rock, angel figurines, a Nativity scene, and the bulletin board or poster board with the words "Jesus is present to us in ordinary things."
5. Gather all the materials for the retreat souvenir and set out on tables in the room that will be used for this activity.
6. Spread out so that at least one team member is greeting the retreatants as they arrive, one is bringing retreatants (and parents) to the gathering room, one is waiting in the gathering room, and one is directing parents and younger siblings to the nursery.
7. Begin the retreat by warmly greeting the retreatants, then introducing the team members.

Gathering Presentation

(The game the children will play is based on the Inquiry model of instruction. The leader describes a seemingly discrepant event and, by asking only "yes" and "no"

138

questions, the children gather enough information to construct an explanation for the event.)

I have a mystery I'd like you to solve. Do you think you can help me? Great.

I'm going to tell you about something very ordinary that happened. This event happened recently, but it has something to do with the birth of Jesus 2,000 years ago. Doesn't that sound mysterious? As you solve the mystery, you'll discover a very powerful explanation for this ordinary event. I'd like you to figure out the story behind this event by asking me questions that I can answer with "yes" or "no." When it sounds like you have gathered enough information to describe the whole story, I'll ask you to give us your explanation. Remember, the mystery has to do with the birth of Jesus, but it's about an event that happened recently. Remember to ask only questions which can be answered with "yes" or "no." Ready?

Here's the story: Maria Carlotta and her friend Carla are friends of Jesus. One day Maria Carlotta called Carla on the phone. After their conversation, Carla took out a tissue to blow her nose. What happened?

Remember, there's a very powerful story behind this one incident, and it has to do with why Jesus was born. By asking me "yes" and "no" questions, see if you can gather enough information to explain the powerful event. Who has a question?

(Following is a sample dialogue which might ensue. The children's questions and responses will vary, of course, but the dialogue is meant to help the leader antici-pate the types of questions that might come up and to equip her with responses that will facilitate the Inquiry process so that the story will successfully come together.)

Child:	Did Carla have a cold?
Leader:	No, she didn't have a cold. *(Repeat each answer in its entirety to reinforce it in the children's minds as they later try to process the information they've gathered.)*
Another Child:	Did Maria Carlotta get mad at Carla on the phone?
Leader:	No, she didn't get angry at her.
Child:	Was Carla crying because she was sad?
Leader:	No, she wasn't crying because she was sad.
Child:	Hmmm. She wasn't sad, she wasn't angry, and she didn't have a cold. Why would she be crying?

Leader:	That's not a "yes" or "no" question. Can you rephrase that? *(The children will frequently forget to phrase their questions to get a "yes" or "no" response.)*
Same Child:	Was Carla crying because...because...hmmm. Because she was happy?
Leader:	Yes! She was crying because she was happy.
Child:	I know. Maria Carlotta told Carla that—
Leader:	Wait a minute. Slow down! We haven't asked enough questions to decide what happened. Let's ask some more "yes" and "no" questions until we get enough information. *(The Inquiry process is not effective if children are allowed to draw conclusions without sufficient data.)*
Same Child:	Did Maria Carlotta call Carla to ask her something?
Leader:	Yes. She called her to ask her something.
Leader:	Why don't we stop for a minute and talk about what we already know. Who can summarize what we've learned so far?
Child (or a combination of several children's contributions):	
	Maria Carlotta called Carla to ask her something, and after they hung up Carla felt so happy it made her cry.
Leader:	Good job. Now I want you to think about *what* Maria Carlotta asked Carla and *why* her question might have made her cry for happiness. Remember, it has to do with why Jesus lived as a human like us, but it happened long after the birth of Jesus. Who has a "yes" or "no" question?
Child:	Did she invite Carla to go somewhere?
Leader:	Yes. Maria Carlotta invited her to come over to her house. *(Answer more than a simple "yes" or "no" in this case in order to move the story along. Where she invited her to go is not important enough to spend more questioning time on. What's important is that she invited Carla to spend time with her.)*
Leader:	Now think about *why* her invitation made her so happy.
Child:	Did Maria Carlotta have computer games at her house?
Leader:	She may have, but that's not what made her so happy. Why might her invitation have made Carla happy?

(Continue to answer questions until the children suggest that Carla had been feeling lonely and Maria Carlotta's phone call and invitation had cheered her up.)

Leader:	We know a lot already about this powerful event. Let's summarize again.

Child

(or children): Maria Carlotta called Carla to invite her over, and after they hung up Carla felt so happy it made her cry because she had been very lonely until Maria Carlotta called.

Leader: So far, so good. Now let's think about how I first described this incident. I said, "Maria Carlotta and her friend Carla are friends of Jesus. One day Maria Carlotta called Carla on the phone. After their conversation, Carla took out a tissue to blow her nose. What happened?" We haven't talked yet about what their friendship with Jesus has to do with the powerful story behind this event.

Depending on time constraints, the leader can either accept more "yes" and "no" questions or engage the children in a discussion until the following powerful story emerges:

One day Maria Carlotta was sitting in her quiet bedroom when she began thinking about her friend Carla. She had a strong desire to call her, for no particular reason. She felt in some way that Jesus was telling her to call her friend. Meanwhile Carla was at her house feeling deeply sad. She had no one to play with, and she was remembering her week at school when several of her classmates had made fun of her day after day. To make matters worse, her parents had scolded her for not doing her chores the day before. Carla wasn't sure if anybody even liked her anymore.

After Maria Carlotta's phone call, Carla felt so happy it made her cry. Jesus had shown Carla his love through Maria Carlotta. Maria Carlotta was a messenger of God's love to Carla. All it took to make Carla feel loved was an ordinary phone call.

Congratulations, everyone! You solved the mystery. In fact, this is the very mystery that surrounds the birth of Jesus at Christmas. We refer to Jesus' birth as the Incarnation. Incarnation means that God became one of us. God's son, Jesus, was human and lived on earth just like us. The Incarnation means that God is with us always. Jesus was born on an ordinary night in an ordinary town in an ordinary stable, and all his life while he was doing ordinary things like we do, Jesus was a messenger of God's love to the people he met. In our lives today, Jesus is still a messenger of God's love to us in the ordinary things of life, even in something as ordinary as a telephone call. Because of the birth of Jesus, we're *like* Jesus, and that means we're messengers of God's love to the people in our lives—just as

Jesus was, and just as Maria Carlotta was to Carla. Jesus wants to talk to us. If we're really still, we can hear what Jesus might want to say to us, just as Maria Carlotta knew that Jesus wanted her to share God's love with Carla on the day she was feeling sad.

We have some fun activities to do now. Let me show you what we'll be doing. *(Show the children the souvenir and story, and tell them they'll also be talking to Jesus.)*

Now look at the color of your nametag. *(Have the children leave the room with the team leader who has the same colored nametag.)*

Children's Activities

The following three children's activities run simultaneously, and the children rotate through them until they've been to all three.

Activity 1: Art as Prayer—Retreat Souvenir

The retreatants will make a festive frame from ordinary materials—paper, foil, and string. Participants will pray with art and will become aware that stillness can bring them close to Jesus. By drawing a prayer, they can tell Jesus how they feel, what has happened to them recently, what is bothering them, what they want, or anything else that's on their minds or in their hearts.

As the children create their foil and string frame, talk about the focus of the retreat (p. 136).

Gather participants around the materials table to create their Draw-a-Prayer frames:

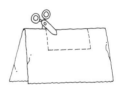

1. The adult leader points out that, just as Jesus is present in the ordinary things of life, prayer goes on in ordinary ways, such as drawing or painting.

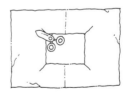

2. Children gently fold back each of the four sections of foil to reveal a 6" opening. They carefully bend the foil between the slanted lines toward the back, first one edge, then a second, a third, and the last side.

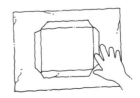

3. Retreatants lay the frame on their drawing paper so they can see how large an area they need to cover.

4. They trace the inside square onto the stiff paper to create a frame.

5. For 10 minutes, children draw whatever they wish on the paper, directing their minds and hearts to God. *(Caution anyone using watercolor paints to use water sparingly. Encourage children to take their time, making sure the pictures are dry before framing them.)*

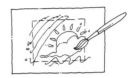
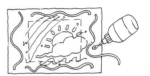

6. The leader plays soft music in the background and encourages children to honor the stillness while they draw.

7. Children can make the frame fancy by placing the string between the paper and the foil to create ridges.

8. With five minutes remaining, retreatants cut their string into four equal pieces by joining the ends together and cutting the fold, then repeating.

9. Children glue the string on the four corners of the frame in spirals, zigzags, or other designs. They gently rub the foil over the top of it to see their design.

10. Participants make the hanger for the back of the finished artwork, using the small piece of foil saved from the cut-out frame. They fold the foil horizontally to a width of 1/2 inch, then form it into a horseshoe shape.

11. With the open end at the bottom, they attach the hanger with tape to the back of the framed artwork, exposing the top loop above the frame.

Announce to the children: It's almost time to move to your next prayer session now. Please help me get ready for the next group by setting up the table the way it was when you arrived. *(Distribute clean paper and foil to each child.)* *(To the final group, give directions about how to put supplies away.)*

Activity 2: Story as Prayer

Story: *Sylvester and the Magic Pebble* by William Steig (New York: Simon & Schuster Inc., 1969)

As the children listen to and discuss the literature, talk about the focus of the retreat (p. 136).

Greet the children.
(As retreatants enter the room, designate a space where they can put their belongings, then invite them to sit where they can see the pictures in the book.)

Raise your hand if you've heard this story before. Wonderful. If you have, let's not tell the others what happens so they can enjoy their experience, too.

This is a time of prayer. Let's get ready to listen to what God wants us to hear in this story. Are you in a comfortable position? Let's all take a deep breath and let it out a little at a time.

Introduce the story.
In a moment of fright, Sylvester the donkey asked his magic pebble to turn him into a rock. He received his wish, but then he couldn't hold the pebble to wish himself back to normal again. Being a rock bought Sylvester plenty of stillness all right—way too much stillness for his liking. Sylvester needed to figure out a way to touch his magic pebble again so he could get out of this jam. Meanwhile, much like Mary and Joseph while Jesus was lost in the Temple, Mr. and Mrs. Duncan were worried sick about their lost son. Let's listen and see if Sylvester is reunited with his parents and restored to his authentic self. Be attentive also to anyone in the story that reminds you of Jesus.

Read the story, taking ample time to show the pictures.
(Using voice intonations, pauses, and a prayerful sense of awe, read the book aloud. Allow time for children to be touched by the words as well as the illustrations. At the conclusion, close the book gently and allow a moment of "think time.")

Talk about the story.
▲ What was Mr. Duncan's pet name for Sylvester? *(our angel)*
▲ Angels are messengers. Was Sylvester a messenger of God's love? Were there others in the story?
▲ And what did Mr. Duncan find? *(a magic red pebble)*
▲ Some people think that God should be like that magic red pebble. They wish God would give them anything they want. If you had your wish, would you ask to be someone different, as Sylvester did?
▲ What gift do you want from Jesus today?
▲ What do you think Jesus would like as a present from you?
▲ Was there anyone in the story that reminded you of Jesus? Tell us what that person did that was like Jesus.

▲ Let's read that last page again, especially the last line. The Duncan Family "had all they wanted." Do you think that being loved by Jesus is a good present? Is there something you would like more? *(Affirm all answers.)* Sometimes it takes a time of stillness like we're having at this retreat to realize what's really important to us.

(Hold up the book with the cover facing the children.) When you're telling your family about the book you read during the retreat today, remember this title. Let's say it together: *Sylvester and the Magic Pebble.*

Announce to the children: It's time to move to your next retreat session now. Be sure to take any of your belongings with you on your way out. Let's walk together.

Alternate Story

If the first choice of literature is unavailable, substitute *Wilfrid Gordon McDonald Partridge* by Mem Fox (New York: Kane/Miller: Brooklyn, 1985).

Introduction:

Wilfrid knew all the people in the old folks' home next door, but he especially liked Miss Nancy, age ninety-six, because she had four names like he did. He asked the residents about *memory* since his parents said Miss Nancy had lost hers. Their replies varied. Wilfrid heard that memory was something "warm," "from long ago," "that makes you cry," "that makes you laugh," "as precious as gold."

Reading:

(Throughout the story, as the two friends bond while recalling ordinary memories, point out how Wilfrid was a messenger of God's love to Miss Nancy.)

Discussion:

▲ Tell about someone you know and like who is over sixty years old and who is a messenger of God's love to you.

▲ Have you had any experience with people in a nursing home or retirement community? Tell us about someone you spoke with there. Did you experience quiet or stillness there?

▲ Talk about how stillness helps us be close to Jesus, allowing us to listen to him. How do you create a place of stillness if you are not alone?

▲ Who in this story reminded you of Jesus?

Activity 3: The Heart Room Prayer

Weave the focus of the retreat throughout the children's experience of the heart room prayer.

(Greet the children as they arrive, then invite them to sit in a circle with you. Be sure the circle is large enough that there is room between the children and they don't touch each other.)

Have any of you ever seen an angel? As you know, there have been television programs and movies about angels. Have you seen any of them? *(Allow 2 or 3 children to share briefly what they've seen.)* If we had an easel and paints here, how would you describe an angel you might paint? *(Encourage a variety of answers. On a blackboard or newsprint, write the key words the participants suggest that are used to describe angels.)* Now that we have some ideas about what an angel might look like, let's think of a job description for an angel. Any ideas? What do you think an angel would actually *do*? *(In a separate column, list the jobs suggested by the children.)*

These are some descriptions of angels and their jobs. The first place we ever heard about angels is in the Bible. Angels are mentioned in the beginning of the Bible, the part we call the Old Testament. Angels are also mentioned in the New Testament during the life of Jesus. We can't see angels. But we can use our imaginations to picture what they might look like. We can also depend on the pictures artists have drawn of angels from their imaginations. But we don't have any actual pictures of angels, or even descriptions of them. Angels existed long before cameras, VCRs, or television.

I'm going to tape these pictures of angels along the walls. *(Tape the pictures at the children's eye level, with enough room between them so the children can stand before the picture of their choice.)* Take time and look over each of the pictures. Notice the way the different artists have drawn the angel in the picture. Would you go and stand in front of the picture that most closely resembles what you think an angel would look like? *(Allow time for children to decide. Several may stand in front of the same picture.)*

Now would you please come back and sit in our circle? Listen first to these two sentences about angels and decide which one you agree with. I'll repeat the sentences, then you can raise your hand at the end of the sentence you agree with. Here's the first sentence: We know exactly what an angel looks like. Here is the second sentence: We do not know exactly what an angel looks like. Raise your hand after the one you agree with. *(Repeat, allowing time after each for the children to raise their hands.)*

How about these choices? First sentence: We know what angels do. Second sentence: We don't know what angels do. Raise your hand after the one you agree with. *(Repeat, allowing time after each for the children to raise their hands.)* Some of us are pretty sure what angels do; some of us aren't sure. Let's look at our list again. *(Refer to the blackboard or newsprint.)*

While it's true we don't know what angels look like for sure, we do know what angels do. Every time we read of an angel appearing in the Bible, the angel is there to deliver a message or to speak for God. The real job of an angel is to be a messenger from God. *(If it's not already on the list, write "messenger" in large letters.)*

Does this look familiar to you? *(Hold up the telephone.)* What does a phone do for us every day? *(Accept answers. Elicit responses such as "Makes communication easier"; "Helps people stay in touch"; "A way to get information we need.")* When a phone call comes in for your parents, brothers, or sisters, what do you do? Right! You take a message. *(Hold up the answering machine.)* Do any of you have one of these in your home? Some of us have it built into our telephones. What's the job of this machine? *(Elicit answers around message-taking.)* Have you seen one of these? *(Hold up the beeper.)* What's the job of this machine? Right. People can leave messages on it.

These machines all have something in common. They help us receive messages. But the most important messengers are not machines at all. They're angels, messengers from God.

Remember when I told you that we first heard about angels in the Bible? I would like to read to you something from the New Testament, something you'll be hearing a lot this Christmas season. It's from the gospel of Luke and it tells us about Jesus' birthday. As I read this, listen closely because angels are mentioned four times. Listen, and pick out what the angel does in Luke's gospel. Look around at the pictures of the angels on the walls and see which one you would choose to put in the gospel. *(Slowly read Luke 2:8-20. Emphasize verses 9, 10, 13, 15, and 17.)*

"That night in the fields near Bethlehem some shepherds were guarding their sheep. All at once an angel came down to them from the Lord, and the brightness of the Lord's glory flashed around them. The shepherds were frightened. But the angel said, 'Don't be afraid! I have good news for you, which will make everyone happy. This very day in King David's hometown a Savior was born for you. He is Christ the Lord. You will know who he is, because you will find him dressed in baby clothes and lying on a bed of hay.'

"Suddenly many other angels came down from heaven and joined in praise of God. They said: 'Praise God in heaven! Peace on earth to everyone who pleases God.'

"After the angels had left and gone to heaven, the shepherds said to each other, 'Let's go to Bethlehem and see what the Lord has told us about.' They hurried off and found Mary and Joseph, and they saw the baby lying on a bed of hay.

"When the shepherds saw Jesus, they told his parents what the angel had said about him.

"Everyone listened and was surprised. But Mary kept thinking about all this and wondering what it meant.

"As the shepherds returned to their sheep, they were praising God and saying wonderful things about him. Everything they had seen and heard was just as the angel had said."

What did the angel do? Did you notice what Luke wrote? *"I proclaim to you good news of great joy."* To proclaim means to tell or to announce. This is what a messenger does. He or she brings good news. At the end, Luke said, *"They made known the message that had been told them about the child."* If the shepherds made known the message, that means they told someone else. They told other people about Jesus. In this way, they were also like angels.

Would you believe me if I told you that each of you is an angel? Does that seem strange to you? *(Encourage comments by children.)* Well, you really are an angel whenever you remind others about Jesus. You do that every time you are kind to someone else. You're like an angel when you're honest and let people know they can count on you, because you're sending the message that Jesus is like this, too. You're an angel whenever you do something to make someone's life better, because you're bringing the message that Jesus is there to help them. When you see another child in trouble and you try to help, you're giving the message that you care about them just the way Jesus cares about them. You've made their life better by trying to help.

I'd like to show you a way you can pray and talk with Jesus. It's important to know, though, that Jesus isn't somewhere far away. Jesus lives within each one of us, in a place deep inside. I call this place the heart room. Your heart room is a place where it's quiet, where you can go anytime you want to and place yourself in the presence of Jesus, your friend.

It helps me to close my eyes and tune out any sounds. Let's all close our eyes. Don't worry that you'll be the only one. I'll keep my own eyes open to make sure it's safe for everyone. All of us have our eyes closed so we won't be distracted.

I'll lead you now through some helps for praying in our heart room. First, take a deep breath to help you relax. Fine. Let's take another deep breath. We all have our eyes closed. As I lead you through this type of prayer please use my suggestions to make pictures in your mind.

Imagine yourself going to a place deep inside yourself. *(Pause.)* You're in your heart room now. Someone just walked into the room, our heart room. It's Jesus. *(Pause.)* What does he look like? What color is his hair? Is it curly? Straight? Long? Short? *(Pause.)* Now look at his face. Is he smiling? How does he look at you? *(Pause.)* When you look at his face do you feel peaceful, happy? What are your feelings when you look at Jesus' face? How is Jesus dressed? What color is his skin?

Jesus sits down next to you. *(Pause.)* Make yourself comfortable next to Jesus. He's there only for you. Talk to Jesus about your desire to be an angel for him. How might you be a messenger to someone else in the coming week to let them know that Jesus loves them very much? What would you like to say to Jesus about this? In our heart room, we don't have to worry that we might say the wrong thing or that Jesus might not understand us. Knowing we're with such an incredibly good friend, let's take a minute to talk with Jesus right now. I'll stop for a short time and you can tell Jesus what person you'd like to be an angel for, and what you would like to do for this person. Jesus might also want to say something to you, too. So listen...

(Wait 60 seconds.)

It's time to go now. Say goodbye to Jesus in whatever way you'd like. Wave, hug him, or say some simple words. *(Pause.)* Tell Jesus you'll come back to your heart room again. *(Pause.)* Now imagine yourself walking back to our room here. *(Pause.)*

When you're ready, please open your eyes.

Sometimes it helps to look back on what happened in prayer in our heart rooms. How did you feel when you were in your heart room? Did you have an easy time talking to Jesus? Do you believe he heard you? Did Jesus say anything to you? Sometimes we hear Jesus and sometimes we don't. That's natural. *(Allow children time to share as they desire.)*

Now that you've had a chance to talk to Jesus in your heart room, you can do this anytime you want. There's no place off-limits for talking to Jesus, no time that's too early or too late. This prayer can be repeated anytime you'd like to talk to Jesus. It's been a good, peaceful place, hasn't it?

Remember what we did here in our retreat. Next time the telephone rings *(hold up the phone)* and you are asked to take a message, think of the angel and how you can be a good-news messenger to someone else. Next time you go home and check your messages *(hold up the answering machine)*, remember that you bring people messages about the goodness of Jesus by treating them kindly. If you see someone answer this *(hold up the beeper)*, remember they are receiving a message. This can be a reminder to you of the good messages you can give other children. When you treat them fairly or include them when you play, they know you and Jesus love them.

I hope you have many happy and prayerful times with Jesus in your heart room when you pray this way again.

Snack
angel-shaped cookies
milk

Adult-Child Sharing Time
After the adult session, parents or adult retreat leaders join their children in the snack room to begin their sharing time. If weather permits, retreatants can go outside for a nature walk. If not, they might want to find a corner to sit in, take a walk through the church, spread out blankets throughout the room, or even create forts out of blankets to sit in for privacy. We allow approximately twenty minutes for adult-child sharing time, asking all participants to return to the gathering room at the allotted time for our closing.

The questions on p. 214 can facilitate adult-child sharing.

If time remains, parents or adult leaders can help children compose a song to the tune of a familiar Christmas carol, using the concepts of the retreat.

For example:
(To the tune of "O Come, All Ye Faithful")

> O, Jesus is present,
> Present in our lives.
> O, he is a gift to us

A messenger of love.
We are his presence
In the world to others.
O, we are his presence
O, we are his presence
O, we are his presence
Each time we love.

(To accommodate children who are not auditory learners, display the lyrics of each song on a large poster board.)

Closing Prayer

The children can close with song, teaching each other the lyrics their group composed, or singing familiar Christmas carols. Following the prayer of joyful song, an adult facilitator leads the children in the following litany:

Adult: I invite all of you to join me in prayer. First, I'll say something to Jesus for all of us. Then you say, "You are with us always."

Adult: Jesus our friend, you lived as a human just like us.

Children: You are with us always.

Adult: Jesus our friend, as a person living among us, you were able to show us God's love.

Children: You are with us always.

Adult: Jesus our friend, you are present to us now in the ordinary things of life.

Children: You are with us always.

Adult: Jesus our friend, you speak to us in our hearts.

Children: You are with us always.

Adult: Jesus our friend, we will be still more often this Christmas so we can listen to you.

Children: You are with us always.

Invite children to join hands and say the Our Father.

Outlines for Parent Sessions

Parent Session 1: Eucharist

Note: The following parent talk is a basic outline with anecdotes, examples, points to expand, and questions to facilitate group interaction. It probably contains more material than can be used. The director, therefore, should remain flexible and make changes according to the time limit of the adult retreat session. We recommend further that the director adapt the outline with personal examples, anecdotes relevant to the participants, and a style of delivery that is natural for the director.

Focus

A parent's involvement in helping a child prepare for first Eucharist is vital. Whether it is deliberate or unconscious, a parent's faith in Jesus and understanding of the Eucharist influences a child's growth in faith. Sacramental preparation for children, therefore, is complete only to the extent that we nurture the spiritual formation of parents as well. An experience of intimacy with Jesus in retreat, along with the support of catechists and other parents, provides spiritual nourishment to parents in their sacred role of accompanying their children on this faith journey.

Eucharist is the center of our faith as believers in Jesus. It is the great act of worship for the God we love, given to us by Jesus at the last supper. The word "Eucharist" means "thanksgiving." Eucharist is our coming together as a community to give thanks to our loving God in Jesus for God's presence with us in all of life. In the Eucharist, Jesus living and present gives himself to us under the appearance of bread and wine. When we receive Jesus we become one with him and with all believers.

Through the Eucharist, we are one in Jesus, all members of the Body of Christ. Gathering together is a reminder that Jesus is present with us, uniting us as brothers and sisters. A growing acceptance and welcome of each other flows out of our unity with Jesus and with one another in Eucharist.

Eucharist is a meal, spiritual and emotional nourishment taken in the company of one another. Jesus himself is our food, the real food and drink of everlasting life that nourishes the deepest part of ourselves. Each of us has received an invitation to this union with Jesus in Eucharist through Jesus' own words: Take and eat. Take and drink (Mk. 14:22-25).

Jesus' sacrifice of the Cross, his total gift of self in love to God for us, is made present in each Eucharistic celebration. In the Eucharist, Jesus is present in his loving offering to God and to us. We can unite our lives with his in our own loving offering to God for others.

In Eucharist we choose to open ourselves to the presence of the Risen Jesus with us and to experience him in this gathering. We listen to Jesus speak to us in the words of scripture and we respond in song and prayer. We receive Jesus in the bread and wine transformed into his Body and Blood. Now present within us in holy communion, Jesus is united with us. We speak our hearts to Jesus and share that presence with one another and with a world in need.

Introductions

As you introduce yourself today, tell who you are and share with each other your response to this question:

▲ How good are you at saying thanks?

Outline

A. Eucharist is the center of our faith life as believers in Jesus.

  1. Eucharist means "thanksgiving." It is the great action in which we worship our loving God.

  2. We give thanks for life, for each other, for forgiveness, for children, for the earth, and for God's presence with us in all of life.

     Anecdote: A young boy being raised lovingly by his grandparents hugged each one every morning and said, "Thank you for taking care of me." Neither of the grandparents had ever taught him this. It was his own idea. In this family, an "attitude of gratitude" reigned. The appreciation exchanged between the boy and his grandparents parallels the gratitude we have in Eucharist for God's presence to us throughout life.

  3. At the last supper Jesus said, "Do this in remembrance of me" (Lk. 22:19). We follow his command at each Eucharistic gathering.

     Expand: Think of a time when—or imagine a time when—you knew you wouldn't be seeing someone you loved for a long time, or ever again. Reflect on what promises you made or would make to that person. When we love someone deeply, his or her absence gives depth to the rituals we continue after they're gone.

Anecdote: A man named Doug tells of watching his father die over several months. In an effort to bring his dad peace, Doug promised to take care of some unfinished business that his father worried about. Still, his father seemed to hang on to life in a state of unrest. Doug realized what his father's deepest wish really was when he uttered these words towards the end of his life: "Doug, make sure your mother has plenty of help. Maybe you can come up with a plan for that." Doug carried out his dad's wish for unity and caring in the family. All family members followed Doug's leadership with added zeal, realizing even deeper meaning to their love, as a memory of their dad.

Share, exchanging responses with two or three others:
▲ When you go to Eucharist, for what do you give thanks?

B. Eucharist is a gathering.
  1. As believing women, men, and children, we gather in Jesus' name: all races, ages, personalities, and states of life. We come together to give thanks.
  2. We are one in Jesus through that gathering, all members of the Body of Christ with Jesus, our head.
  3. Our gathering is a constant reminder that we are all sisters and brothers of Jesus who is present with us.
  4. We grow in unity with each other by our welcome and acceptance of one another as well as our reverence for Jesus who is present with us.

Expand: Consider the home, where the daily gathering of family members can be a constant challenge to growth in unity. In her book *Traits of the Healthy Family,* Dolores Curran cites acceptance of differences in each other as a quality of healthy families. So, too, our church is healthy to the extent that all members are valued for their uniqueness. The Eucharist is a reminder to us that all members are united by virtue of Christ's presence in each one.

Share, exchanging responses with two or three others:
▲ In what ways have you been welcomed or not welcomed into the group at a Sunday Eucharist?
▲ In what ways have you welcomed others into the community?
▲ If your experience has not been positive, what did you learn from it about what Eucharist *should* be?

C. Eucharist is a meal.

1. We come to a meal to be nourished with food and drink, and to be nourished emotionally and spiritually in the company of one another.

Expand: Families can give depth to the "meal" dimension of Eucharist. As children get older, schedules can begin to interfere with the evening mealtime gathering. However, helping children understand the significance of the Eucharist as a meal where emotional and spiritual nourishment takes place is more effective if they have family meals as a frame of reference.

Anecdote: A family had moved to a new state and greatly missed their relatives and friends, who had provided a strong support system for them. They had no family in their new location, and friends were slow in coming as they discovered that many of their neighbors were gone most of the day. Unexpectedly, they soon found themselves with nourishment that equaled and in some ways surpassed what they'd known back home: the spiritual and emotional nourishment of their parish community, which they discovered as they gradually took part in activities. The Sunday Eucharist reminded this family of their unity with each other and with Jesus.

2. Jesus promised that those who come to him will never thirst (Jn. 4:10).
3. Jesus has extended a personal invitation to each of us: Take and eat. Take and drink (Mk. 14:22-25).
4. In Eucharist we receive Jesus, the food and drink of everlasting life.
5. Jesus himself is the bread of life, "real food" that nourishes the deepest part of ourselves (Jn. 6:51).
6. He invites all people to this banquet.

Share, exchanging responses with two or three others:

▲ What experiences have you had as an adult that help you realize what Jesus is offering you in this meal, the Eucharist?

▲ What ties have you found between the Eucharist and the family meal?

D. Eucharist is a sacrifice.

1. A sacrifice is a special offering, a gift of self to God.

Expand: The concept of sacrifice has too often been confused with suffering in the Christian tradition. While sacrifice might involve suffering, suffering is not always a sacrifice. Sacrifice is an attitude of self-giving. For the one who sacrifices, everything is done for the greater honor and glory of God. From Jesus to St. Paul to Mother Teresa, those who give themselves totally to God have said: "God is everything to me. All that I am is for God." In this sense, the Christian life is one of sacrifice, even in the absence of suffering.

2. Jesus' life and suffering death were a total gift of self in love to God for us.

3. Jesus' sacrifice of the cross is renewed and commemorated in each Eucharistic celebration.

4. In the Eucharist, Jesus is present in his loving offering of himself to the Father and to us.

5. We can unite our lives with his in our own loving offering to God for others.

Expand: The power of this renewal of Jesus' sacrifice in each celebration of Eucharist is difficult to overstate. Each celebration brings encouragement for our total giving of self to God, in whatever form that takes in our own lives. United in Christ's sacrifice, we go forth to share ourselves with all of God's people for the building of the kingdom. This giving of self begins in the family.

The sacrifice of family members to each other must model itself after the generous and healthy self-giving of Jesus to God and God's people so that our sacrifice doesn't turn into co-dependence or martyrdom, destructive to all. In his ministry, for example, Jesus knew when to be present and when he needed to go away from the crowds. Consider this account from Mark: *"But so many people were coming and going that Jesus and the apostles did not even have a chance to eat. Then Jesus said, 'Let's go to a place where we can be alone and get some rest.' They left in a boat to a place where they could be alone. But many people saw them leave and figured out where they were going. So people from every town ran on ahead and got there first"* (Mk. 6:31-33). Our own sacrifice to each other cannot be a loving and generous self-giving if we don't occasionally nourish and replenish our spirit, as Jesus did.

Anecdote: A mother of thirteen gave a talk to a women's spirituality group composed mostly of mothers of young children. Her advice was, "Take time for yourself every day, even if it's only five minutes." Many of the listeners groaned inwardly. "Five minutes will do nothing for me," one mother finally blurted out. A suffering mother cannot be a welcome gift to her family. Other family members, too, should understand the purity of intention involved in sacrifice, modeled by Jesus. Begrudgingly giving or doing in the name of self-giving can divide rather than unite a family.

156

Share, exchanging your responses with two or three others:

▲ What might your offering of self be to your family, co-workers, or the world?

▲ In what small ways can we instill in our families a sense of loving sacrifice?

E. Eucharist is the presence of the risen Jesus with us.

Expand: The liturgy follows the dynamic of love that facilitates our becoming one with the risen Jesus.

1. In Eucharist we make a choice to meet the risen Jesus, to open ourselves to him, and to experience him in this gathering.
2. We listen to Jesus speak to us in the words of scripture.
3. We respond to his living Word with song, prayer, and gifts.
4. We receive the risen Jesus present in the bread and wine now transformed into his Body and Blood.
5. We speak our hearts to Jesus present within us in holy communion.
6. We share that presence with one another and a world in need.

Share

▲ Describe a special experience of Jesus' presence within you. Reflect back on this time, and write your response in a notebook or journal. Then share with the whole group, as you desire.

Conclusion: During the upcoming week, reflect on this question:

▲ For what will I give thanks next Sunday at Eucharist?

Parent Session 2: Reconciliation

Note: The following parent talk is a basic outline with anecdotes, examples, points to expand, and questions to facilitate group interaction. It probably contains more material than can be used. The director, therefore, should remain flexible and make changes according to the time limit of the adult retreat session. We recommend further that the director adapt the outline with personal examples, anecdotes relevant to the participants, and style of delivery that fits the director.

Focus

As believers in Jesus, we know through God's Word, through the teaching of the Church, and through our own experience, that God is always with us. (*"The Lord is good! [God's] love and faithfulness will last forever!"* Psalm 100:5.) We respond to God by living our lives in truth and love. Yet every human being experiences failure and brokenness.

We fail endlessly and know the guilt and alienation that our sin causes. Our brokenness separates us from God and from one another. Our sin is magnified in our communities and world by our failure to speak and act for justice and to care for the poor. Yet God's Word to us has always been one of forgiveness and peace. (*"I will listen to you, Lord God, because you promise peace to those who are faithful..."* Psalm 85:8.)

The capacity to choose is one of God's greatest gifts to us. The ten commandments, the great commandment of Jesus, and the teachings of the church provide guidelines for loving choices, because the will of God is that we live in honesty and love with God and each other. God has promised to be with each of us in the bittersweetness of life, and God's will is to bring us to Jesus in the fullness of life, not only in eternity, but now. Even in our poor choices, our sinful choices, God wills to forgive us and restore us to this fullness of life.

God's message in the Hebrew scriptures was repeatedly one of mercy and forgiveness. God promised to be with Israel in all the hardships and setbacks of life. God's mercy and forgiveness were not worn out by human sinfulness and failure. Then as now, God's mercy is everlasting.

Jesus is God's message of forgiveness and reconciliation enfleshed. Jesus invited all persons into God's Kingdom. He spread the message of peace by word and example as he loved and forgave endlessly during his life. In the end, because he hung from the cross enduring a painful, humiliating death for us, we are now reconciled with God.

Reconciliation is a sacrament of peace, one of the Church's great signs that Christ is acting directly in our lives. In this sacrament, as we name our sins, express sorrow, and hear the words of absolution spoken by the priest, we experience the mercy and acceptance of God. The only unforgivable sin is acting on the belief that our sin and brokenness are greater than God's mercy and forgiveness.

The home is the school of forgiveness. Here, children learn mercy and the give-and-take of forgiving one another. In taking seriously God's relationship with Israel and Jesus' compassion with God's people, then modeling this reconciliation in their homes, parents have the sacred role of teaching their children the depth of God's forgiveness.

Introductions

Tell us who you are and share with us your response to this question:

> ▲ What is your hope for your child as s/he prepares for the sacrament of Reconciliation?

Outline

A. The capacity to choose is one of God's greatest gifts to women and men.

   1. Our God desires only our good.

   2. The will of God is to be with each of us in the bittersweetness of life and to bring us to Jesus now and in eternity.

   Expand: Think how often we heard the promise that our reward would come in heaven. The good news is that God wants fullness of life for us now. While God never promised to spare us from the human condition, God did promise to be with us always.

   Anecdote: Gretchen and Tomas trusted God to guide them in their decisions. They were disillusioned, then, when they accepted a job transfer that resulted in much heartbreak. Life in the new town, as well as the job itself, were filled with sadness and disappointment right from the start. If God wants fullness of life, they wondered, why are we hurting so much? The answer to their dilemma came quite undramatically. No spectacular miracles snatched them from their misery and placed them in bliss. Instead, they stayed in their new location and struggled with the job. But in the midst of their burden, they felt a sense of peace, a certitude about what they were doing which they ascribe to God's comfort and care for them. "It's not easy to explain," commented Gretchen. "God truly does make our life better. Not that we didn't kick and scream about our situation. But God responded with love."

   3. God asks us to live in honesty and love.

   4. The great commandment, the ten commandments, the teachings of the Church guide us in how to live in Jesus' way.

   5. Even with our poor choices, our sinful choices, God wills to forgive and restore us.

   Expand: The source of much suffering in the world is precisely the misuse of our freedom to choose. In exercising this choice, we have potential to hurt ourselves and others. Yet God always forgives, recognizing our brokenness as well as our great ability to love. God's immediate forgiveness heals our woundedness and frees us to live a more loving life.

   Anecdote: In healthy families, members forgive each other without revenge. However, this is the ideal, and quite difficult for many of us. As a parent, Greg wrestles with his desire, but seeming inability, to forgive unconditionally. His own parents left him groveling each time they "forgave" him, and he finds himself wanting others to suffer in the same way when they've offended him. A turning point for Greg came when his ten-year-old daughter forgave him without hesitation, when he broke a promise to her. What he noticed in this reconciliation was a desire within himself to never hurt her again. His daughter's unconditional forgiveness was an occasion of healing for him.

Share with one other person:

▲ How have your experiences of forgiving and being forgiven affected your understanding of God's forgiveness?

B. God's message in the Hebrew scriptures is one of mercy and forgiveness.
   1. Ours is a God of mercy and forgiveness (Ps. 103:17).
   2. Israel testifies to God's mercy and forgiveness (Ps. 86:5).
   3. God's mercy is poured out on all, the deserving and the undeserving: Sarah, Hagar, and Abraham; Rebecca and Isaac; Leah, Rachel, and Jacob; David; all of Israel in her sinfulness.
   4. God does not test Israel nor cause her misfortunes. Rather, God promises to be with her in all the hardships and setbacks of life (Isa. 43:1-5a).
   5. In the face of Israel's unfaithfulness God promises, *"I, the Lord, invite you to come and talk it over. Your sins are scarlet red, but they will be whiter than snow or wool"* (Isa. 1:18).
   6. God's mercy and forgiveness are not worn out by human sinfulness and failure. God's mercy is everlasting. As the psalmist says, *"The Lord is always kind to those who worship him, and he keeps his promises to their descendants..."* (Ps. 103:17).
   7. The great story of God's forgiveness in the Hebrew scriptures is that of Hosea. *(Take time to tell this story of the faithful Hosea and Gomer, his wife, a prostitute who returned again and again to lovers. Each time God tells Hosea to take her back, to restore her as his wife.)* This is the story of God and us.

Reflect, then write your response in a notebook or journal.

▲ What does the story of Hosea and Gomer say about God's forgiveness of you?

C. Jesus is God's message of forgiveness and reconciliation enfleshed.
   1. All are invited into God's kingdom: the just and the sinner, the healthy, the lame, and the halt.
   2. All persons have worth (Lk. 19:1-10).

3. In answer to Peter's question about how many times we can hope to be forgiven, Jesus answered, "Seventy times seven."

4. Jesus said "Peace be with you" 165 times in the gospels.

5. A wonderful example of Jesus' forgiveness was his response to the woman caught in adultery. Not only did Jesus forgive and restore the woman, but he also showed mercy to the Pharisees who accused her only to trick Jesus, giving them the chance to be reconciled with God as well (Jn. 8:1-11).

6. On the cross Jesus himself begged, *"Father, forgive them"* (Lk. 23:24).

7. Through Jesus' selfless love in enduring a painful, humiliating death for us, we are reconciled with God.

Share, exchanging responses with two or three others:

▲ Recall a time in your life when you experienced the peace of Jesus' mercy and forgiveness.

D. Reconciliation is a sacrament of peace.

1. One of the church's signs of Christ acting directly in our lives is the sacrament of Reconciliation.

2. Through this sacrament of forgiveness, we experience God's mercy and acceptance.

3. Jesus' parable of the father who welcomed his prodigal son (Lk. 15:11-32) teaches us God's acceptance and forgiveness for each of us as we celebrate this sacrament.

Expand: Because this parable is so familiar, we risk tuning out its message as we hear it one more time. Some people report powerful experiences when they pray this parable as a contemplation in the Ignatian tradition. In contemplation, we allow the Spirit to bring us into the story, either as one of the characters or as a bystander. We use all our senses to become part of the mystery in contemplation, where the spirit of Jesus teaches us as he did his disciples. To lead retreatants in contemplation, follow these steps:

▲ Invite retreatants to assume a comfortable position, then close their eyes to prepare for the reading.

▲ Instruct retreatants to enter into the scene and listen to what each person is saying. Tell them to use the other senses to get a feel of the setting and ambience.

▲ Explain that they should allow the Spirit to help them take the part of one character in the scene.

▲ Allow participants a few moments to quiet and center themselves.

▲ Slowly, expressively read the passage.

▲ Allow approximately two minutes of quiet time for the retreatants to remain in the scene.

▲ Encourage participants to reflect on this question: What difference does the message I heard make in my life? Allow a minute more of silence.

▲ Lead retreatants out of prayer gradually, encouraging them to close their time in prayer in whatever way they'd like. Invite them to open their eyes when they're ready.

4. Naming sins, sorrow for sins, and hearing the words of absolution are essential to the sacrament of Reconciliation.

5. The only unforgivable sin is acting on the belief that our sin and brokenness are greater than God's mercy and forgiveness.

6. The home is the school of forgiveness, where children and parents learn of mercy in the give-and-take of ongoing forgiveness of one another.

Expand: Arguments are inevitable when people live in intimacy. Children actually benefit from hearing their parents resolve conflict, which provides a model of reconciliation for children. In embracing conflict, children see it not as something destructive to be avoided, but as a pathway to more honest and loving relationships. By extension, living a life of reconciliation opens the way to an honest and loving relationship with God.

Anecdote: One Mother's Day, a woman expressed hope that the family might go on a picnic together. Her daughter begged off, asking if she could instead go to the mall with her friend. The mother was horrified that her daughter would make such a request on Mother's Day. After some unpleasant negotiation, the family decided to go on the picnic without the daughter, who would stay home and catch up on homework. A few hours later, the family returned home, and the daughter was gone. Within minutes, the phone rang. The daughter was calling from the mall, asking for a ride home. The mother jumped in the car and fumed all the way to the mall until, by the time she reached her destination, she could hardly contain herself. A torrent of condemnations fell on the daughter: "How dare you disobey me? What kind of daughter would go to the mall instead of spending time with her mother on Mother's Day?" The daughter apologized repeatedly, but the mother's anger blocked her ability to hear. When they pulled up in front of their home, the daughter apologized once again and handed her mother a package from the mall. "I'm sorry, Mom. I wanted to get you a Mother's Day present," she said sadly as she got out of the car.

By God's grace, mother and daughter reconciled that afternoon. The daughter recognized how her way of surprising her mother had backfired, actually hurting her mother. The mother realized how important it is to try to understand a child's motivation when s/he seems to be acting out. And both came to understand the power of reconciliation. Their reconciliation restored peace, and paved the way for a more open, honest, loving relationship with each other.

Reflect, considering this question in the week ahead:

▲ Do my loved ones experience God's mercy and forgiveness from me? If so, how? If not, why?

Parent Session 3: Interior Transformation—An Unfolding

Note: The following parent talk is a basic outline with anecdotes, examples, points to expand, and questions to facilitate group interaction. It probably contains more material than can be used. The director, therefore, should remain flexible and make changes according to the time limit of the adult retreat session. We recommend further that the director adapt the outline with personal examples, anecdotes relevant to the participants, and style of delivery that fits the director.

Focus

God wills happiness and wholeness for us. Yet happiness often eludes us, for several reasons. One barrier is our own brokenness, resulting in the fear that we don't deserve happiness. Another is the impact of our failures on our sense of inner peace. We find ourselves "waiting for the other shoe to fall." A third barrier to happiness and wholeness is that suffering is an inevitable part of life. Some people clearly suffer more than others, while some *perceive* suffering to a greater degree than others. Though suffering is inevitable, God does not will suffering. Healthy spirituality reflects the words of Jesus: "I came so that everyone would have life, and have it in its fullest" (Jn. 10:10). To live our call as followers of Jesus, our spiritual journey must be a journey towards happiness and wholeness.

The spiritual journey is one of interior transformation, and the results of interior transformation are spiritual and emotional wholeness. If our life brings only suffering in place of happiness and wholeness, then change needs to come about. When we pray for our life to change, God often answers by changing us. Because the Holy Spirit dwells within us, God does God's work of transformation from within. When we place ourselves in God's tender care, when we center ourselves in God each day in prayer, we find the conditions most conducive to our growth and transformation: unconditional love, endless mercy and compassion, eternal care. The love relationship we have with God is transforming.

The greatest barrier to our wholeness is trying to conform to external standards while ignoring the stirrings of the Spirit within, who is leading us to authenticity. Many of us have spent a lifetime trying to conform to the external demands of our environment: our family, peers, society, world, possibly even our church. But Paul advises us to give up our old ways and become like God, as we were created to be, a gradual growth towards authenticity that can be painful. But as we are transformed into our authentic selves, we find freedom.

Daily prayer facilitates our growth into authenticity. Each time we turn our hearts to God through prayer, we center ourselves in the Spirit of God, who dwells within. God's Spirit is all love, peace, joy, patience, kindness, goodness, faithfulness, gentleness, and self-control, and we ourselves have the potential to manifest these qualities of God. As we are transformed we become more like God, who dwells within. We are freer, more authentic, whole.

Outline

God wills happiness and wholeness for us.

Expand: Unfortunately, some people cannot seem to find a place of happiness and wholeness. Several factors contribute to this. For some, the trials of life can be relentless. For others, the *perception* that life holds pain can block happiness. Our own brokenness can also sabotage happiness, as can the mistaken belief that Christianity requires suffering.

A. Healthy spirituality requires us to let go of the notion that suffering is our fate as Christians.

1. Suffering is an inevitable part of life. We suffer because of illness and psychological woundedness in ourselves and others, and because of people's misguided use of free will. But God does not will suffering, and God does not cause suffering to test us.

Examples: Cancer, AIDS, or other devastating illnesses are not of God's making. Nor are abuse or death from tragic causes. God did not promise to spare us from the human condition; God promised to be with us through it all.

2. Jesus said, "I came so that everyone would have life, and have it in its fullest" (Jn. 10:10). Fullness of life necessarily includes happiness and wholeness.

Anecdote: A woman who complained of chronic pain, illness, persecution by others, and depression, once said, "I think some people are called to suffer. And I think I'm one of them." One way to discern whether the suffering is sanctifying or spiritually destructive is to examine these questions:

▲ Does my suffering in any way give life to others? Or does it deal death to myself and those I encounter?

▲ Do I radiate God to others in my suffering? Or am I the antithesis of love, peace, joy, patience, kindness, and goodness?

3. To live our call as followers of Jesus, our spiritual journey must be a journey towards wholeness.

B. Spiritual and emotional wholeness are the results of interior transformation.
1. If our life brings suffering in place of happiness and wholeness, then change is in order.
2. On the spiritual journey, positive, lasting change moves from inside out.
3. Because the Holy Spirit dwells within us, God does God's work of transformation from within.

C. Interior transformation is an unfolding.
1. An anonymous source says, "Children are not things to be molded, but people to be unfolded."
2. The mystic Therese of Lisieux refers to us as beauty in God's garden.

Anecdote: Notice how flowers bloom into their beauty. We plant them in environments of soil, sun, and water that are conducive to their particular growth, then watch them unfold. We don't mold them. In fact, we can't. It is the same with children. Each child is unique, each requiring varying doses and styles of attention, affection, and direction. Even when parents attempt to mold children, they eventually find their way to personal authenticity, sometimes painfully.

3. If we place ourselves in God's tender care, by centering ourselves in God each day in prayer, we've found the conditions most conducive to our growth and transformation, to our unfolding: unconditional love, endless mercy and compassion, and eternal care.

Share, exchanging responses with one other person:

▲ As a child, was I molded or unfolded? How can I, in imitation of God, help my children unfold? In what way would this look different from molding?

God wills happiness and wholeness for us.

The greatest barrier to our wholeness is trying to conform to external standards while ignoring the stirrings of the Spirit within, who is leading us to authenticity.

A. We've spent a lifetime attempting to "fit in" by conforming to our environment: our family, peers, society, world, possibly even our church.

B. Dying to self means surrendering our self-centered intentions to the transforming power of God.

1. Paul advises us to give up our old ways and become like God, as we were created to be: *"You were told that your foolish desires will destroy you and that you must give up your old way of life with all its bad habits. Let the Spirit change your way of thinking and make you into a new person. You were created to be like God...."* (Eph. 4:22-24).
2. It's a slow, gradual process, and we're tempted to give up.
3. It's often a painful process because we're leaving the familiar for the unfamiliar.

Anecdote: Our lives hold numerous experiences of the discomfort of leaving the familiar for the unfamiliar. One example is the sometimes dramatic adjustment to other cultures. For example, a young college student was preparing to spend a year studying abroad on a scholarship. He had read in detail the brochure his college had issued explaining the phenomenon of culture shock, and he felt ready. But the transition from the familiar to the unfamiliar proved far more difficult, at times nearly devastating, to the young man, and he found himself in a state of depression for several months. His immediate reaction was to find a way to cut his stay short. When this was not possible, he stuck it out and, once over the hump, the college student discovered a wonderful new way of living that transformed him in many ways.

4. As we are transformed into our authentic selves, we find freedom.

C. Daily prayer facilitates our growth into authenticity.
1. Each time we turn our hearts to God through prayer, we center ourselves in the Spirit of God, who dwells within.

2. God's Spirit is all love, peace, joy, patience, kindness, goodness, faithfulness, gentleness, and self-control.

3. Those same fruits are ours because God dwells within. As we give up our old ways, the ones that are not life-giving, we gradually become persons who beautifully manifest the indwelling God in the qualities of love, peace, joy, patience, kindness, goodness, faithfulness, gentleness, and self-control.

Expand: Think of some of the movies where people exchanged "spirits" with another person (e.g., *Freaky Friday, Big, Vice Versa*). These characters found themselves in unpredictable, often comical, situations because they had the inner qualities of someone else. Their lives were suddenly different. For us, though, the transformation is gradual. We become more like God, who dwells within. We are freer, more whole, authentic.

Reflect, writing a brief response in a journal:
▲ What would being whole mean for me?

To tune into your deepest sense of self, ask:
▲ What causes disorder within me? What interior growth or change would bring me fullness of life?

The spiritual journey is one of interior transformation.

A. The love relationship we have with God is transforming.

1. John tells us that God loved us first (1 Jn. 4:10).

Expand: Many of us hesitate to love for fear of rejection. In fact, for most of us, rejection is already a part of our history. But God frees us from that burden. We don't have to initiate the relationship because God first loved us. There is no possibility of rejection.

Anecdote: A woman recalls the experience of being ridiculed during third and fourth grade because of a physical flaw. Mary describes how she felt unlovable during those years, so much so that for two years she hesitated to initiate friendships for fear of rejection. However, she remembers feeling safe and loved during that time when she was with her parents, who perceptively affirmed her in every way. Fortified with the love and acceptance of these two significant people, Mary was further affirmed in fifth grade when a new girl at school approached her and wanted to be her friend. For Mary, the experiences of being loved first, by her parents and then by the new student, were healing and transforming.

2. John further states that we love because God first loved us (1 Jn. 4:11).

Expand: Love is a powerful force that grows and spreads.

Anecdote: A woman was known around her workplace as a strong presence of love and caring. Valerie was a thoughtful listener, a tender shoulder to lean on, and a healing hugger. One day someone asked her where all that love came from. Her answer was unhesitating: "I am totally loved by a lot of people." What a life-giving way to perceive reality. Many of us are totally loved by a lot of people, but we allow our nemeses to cloud the picture. All of us, though, are totally loved by God. This alone can be enough motivation to love others.

3. People who have undergone powerful conversions often refer to an overwhelming sense of being loved or cared for, either from God directly or from people in their lives.

Anecdote: Prisons and hospitals are full of dramatic examples. A more down-to-earth example, however, is the story of a mother of eight who was feeling isolated and unaffirmed and, on this particular evening, exhausted after a full day. As she lay in bed trying to sleep, tears rolled down her cheeks. Her concerned husband asked what was the matter. "I just wish someone would call me sometimes," she said sadly. The next evening at dinner, the family witnessed a transformed mother. Eyes bright, voice light, her words nearly danced across the table: "Three people called me today." The caring of three friends, the love of God through them, were the fuel this mother needed to continue being a presence of love to her family.

B. When we pray for our life to change, God often answers by changing us.

Anecdote: Ming Lo Moves the Mountain by Arnold Lobel (New York: Scholastic, 1982) is a charming story that reflects this theme. Ming Lo and his wife live in a house directly under a mountain, which causes constant rain. They decide they must move the mountain. Ming Lo visits a wise person who gives him advice about how to move the mountain, which includes pushing it with a tree trunk, making baked goods to appease the spirits of the mountain, and a few other unsuccessful suggestions. Nothing works. Finally, the wise person instructs Ming Lo and his wife to take their house apart, pack their belongings, and do the dance of the moving mountain. Ming Lo and his wife are to close their eyes and "dance," putting one foot behind the other. After many hours, they can open their eyes and they'll see that the mountain has moved. There they should rebuild their house.

Share, exchanging responses in the large group:

▲ Is this idea (B, above) true to your experience?

▲ Have you found that your prayers were answered with personal change rather than an altering of external circumstances?

C. When we are transformed, people around us are transformed.

Anecdote: Conrad tells the story of a time during his upbringing when his father's mood swings affected his sense of well-being. He remembers low self-esteem because he perceived the cause of his father's distance to be flaws in himself. The father gradually healed from his woundedness and his relationship with his grown son was renewed. "The ramifications of the change in my father are widespread," says Conrad. "My whole family has been affected by it in different ways. I myself feel more self-love. I don't know why that would be, but it is."

Reflect, considering this question in the week ahead:

▲ Is the love relationship I have with members of my family transforming for them? For me? In what ways?

Parent Session 4: Awareness of God's Presence and Action

Note: The following parent talk is a basic outline with anecdotes, examples, points to expand, and questions to facilitate group interaction. It probably contains more material than can be used. The director, therefore, should remain flexible and make changes according to the time limit of the adult retreat session. We recommend further that the director adapt the outline with personal examples, anecdotes relevant to the participants, and style of delivery that fits the director.

Focus

God promised to be with us always. Jesus sent his Spirit and, as a result, the Spirit of Jesus dwells within us and is present in every aspect of life, unifying us with God and with people, guiding us, and empowering us. Like the sun, God is always there, even when we don't recognize God's presence and action.

We come to see God's unifying Spirit as we recognize that the primary effect of the Holy Spirit acting in us is love. God's Spirit guides us with the gifts of wisdom, understanding, counsel, and knowledge. The Spirit also directs our consciences and illuminates our choices so we can better discern God's will. Our desire to serve God and each other is further evidence of the Spirit. The Holy Spirit empowers us to use the gifts God has given us for the purpose of building up the community.[1]

The inevitable struggles and darknesses in life are challenges to feeling God's presence. A natural part of the spiritual journey, darkness is sometimes accompanied by suffering in life, but not always. Many of the great saints describe such spiritual darkness in which God seems distant or absent. But God isn't. In faith we trust that God is with us always. We can take consolation in the knowledge that the *desire* to feel God comes from God within us. Through prayer, we grow in union to this God within, which gives rise to our sense of connectedness with God. In this way, the presence and action of God in our lives, even during times when that presence is difficult to feel, give us victory over darkness.

The spiritual journey is one of growing in awareness of God's presence and action of God in our lives. God attempts to communicate with us through scripture, insights, people, events, and feelings. God's self-revelation is ongoing—whether we can *feel* it or not.

Everything has the potential to manifest God to us if we're aware. Because most of our life is ordinary, God speaks to us most often in ordinary ways through what is familiar to us. Parents have a wonderful opportunity to share with each other and with their children their own awareness of God's presence and action. God is in the people who surround us, but God can also speak to us from books, movies or television, and nature. Spiritual discernment means recognizing the movement of God's Spirit in our lives.

Outline

Anecdote: Children speak to us of the mysteries of God if we have ears to hear. The following story reflects the spirit of Jesus' invitation and promise to us, as if he were saying, "I want to be a part of your life. I'm here, whether you recognize me or not."

Betsy, Amy, and Paul, all three years old, were playing in Betsy's home. Suddenly all three started screaming and crying, causing Betsy's mother to race to the play room. "What's wrong?" she exclaimed, expecting bruises, breaks, bumps, or even worse child-war casualties.

"B-B-Betsy and Amy won't let me play with them-m-m," sobbed Paul.

"Well," explained Betsy, arms folded, jaw set, "I want to be the mother and Amy wants to be the baby, and there's nothing for Paul to do."

"Now, Betsy," admonished Mom, "you let Paul play with you. The father... Big brother... You can find something for him to do."

"Ohhh-kaaaaay," groaned Betsy reluctantly. Then after a long pause, "You can be the grandma."

Mom smiled and turned to walk upstairs.

"And you died," whispered Betsy to Paul.

Expand: Little Paul was trying desperately to communicate the same message Jesus tells us today: "Hey! Pay attention to me. I'm here whether you acknowledge me or not!" Jesus promised to send his Spirit and, as he promised, the Holy Spirit dwells within each of us. Because of the indwelling Spirit, God is with us always, unifying us, guiding us, and empowering us.

God promised to be with us always.

A. The scriptures bear this out.

    1. "People of Israel... I won't forget you" (Isa. 44:21).

    2. "I will be with you always, even until the end of the world" (Mt. 28:20).

    3. "Then I will ask the Father to send you the Holy Spirit who will help you and always be with you... I won't leave you like orphans. I will come back to you" (Jn. 14:16-18).

    Expand: Jesus' promise is at the heart of our trust that God's presence and action are real in our lives.

B. The Spirit of Jesus infuses every aspect of life.

    Expand: Richard Hauser, S.J., explains beautifully in his book *In His Spirit* how to recognize the presence and action of God's Spirit in our lives. The biggest barrier to this recognition is perceiving God as outside ourselves, "removing God from any real awareness of the presence of the Spirit in human behavior."[2] However, because God's Spirit joins our spirit, God is always with us, working in us.

    1. God's Spirit unifies us with God and with each other in love.

    Expand: The Spirit, joined with our spirit, moves us towards God and others. In fact, the primary effect of the Holy Spirit acting in us is love. We begin to see the Spirit in others. A sign that the Spirit is blocked, on the other hand, is when motives are selfish or actions are begrudging.

2. God's Spirit guides us with the gifts of wisdom, understanding, counsel, and knowledge.

Expand: First, the Holy Spirit enlightens us, enabling us to recognize our love relationship with God. The Spirit also directs our consciences. The guidance of God's Spirit involves a third aspect: the Spirit illuminates our choices so we can better discern God's will.

Anecdote: If parents begin providing their children with the vocabulary to describe experiences of the Spirit, children have a tool for tuning into the stirrings of Spirit as appropriate for their developmental level. Five-year-old Tim, for example, stormed into his house one day, beside himself with good news: "Mom! Mom! Jesus just put six ideas in my head!"

Twelve-year-old Sara found hope upon the death of her grandmother with her insight that her grandmother's spirit might now be present to her in ways similar to Jesus' Spirit. Sixteen-year-old Peggy depended on the Holy Spirit to help her discern choices relevant to her life as a student and teenage friend. All these experiences of the Spirit's gifts were heightened by the children's awareness of Spirit, instilled in them by their parents.

3. God's Spirit empowers us to serve God and each other.

Expand: God gives each of us gifts for the purpose of building up the community. Richard Hauser explains it well: "These gifts, or charisms, transform the natural capacities of the person and enable them to be used more effectively for the good of the whole group."[3]

Expand: The tendency parents have to affirm their children carries spiritual significance in light of this concept. Not only do we point out their gifts because we think they're wonderful people, but we encourage them to use what God gave them to serve each other. Again, if we supply children with the vocabulary of Spirit as we make them aware of their gifts, we equip them with a mindset of service to God and the community.

Share, exchanging responses in a large group:

▲ The home is a community built up with the gifts of each family member. How do you see this happening in your family or in families you've observed?

C. John of the Cross says God is like the sun.

Expand: God's power to warm and heal is always with us. However, there may be times when we're inside with the blinds closed, times when clouds cover the skies, night times, or times when we hide under the shade of a tree. But these times of darkness are only temporary. The sun is always there, perhaps warming the other side of the world, perhaps waiting for a storm to pass, but predictably ready to return to warm and heal once again, as is its function. Because of the sun's constancy, darkness has no lasting power.

Reflect, then write in a journal:

▲ Am I aware of the presence of the Holy Spirit in me? In what way(s)? If not, what barrier might there be to my receiving the Spirit's gifts of unifying, enlightening, and empowering?

The inevitable struggles and darkness in life are challenges to feeling God's presence.

A. Darkness is a natural part of the spiritual journey.

Expand: The experience of darkness on the spiritual journey is described by various people with striking similarities. John of the Cross refers to the night of sense and dark night of the soul; Ignatius of Loyola speaks of desolation; the English mystic Julian of Norwich describes barrenness in prayer; Teresa of Avila, spiritual pain; Therese of Lisieux, a dark tunnel. We also hear of the cross and the desert. For some, darkness comes in the form of aridity, restlessness, or a feeling that there must be something more to life. Thomas Moore, author of *Care of the Soul,* cautions against hiding the dark places of the soul. Caring for the soul means acknowledging darkness, which is at home in the soul.[4]

B. Our sinfulness gives rise to our sense of incompletion, dividedness, isolation, and guilt.

Expand: At times we feel the presence of God, a great gift. Often, however, God seems distant or absent. God is neither. The *desire* to feel God comes from God within us. Through prayer, we grow in union with this God within, which gives rise to our sense of completion, connectedness, unity, and inner freedom.

C. The presence and action of God in our lives gives us victory over darkness.

Expand: Scripture and tradition assure us that grace is more powerful than sin (2 Cor. 12:9). Julian of Norwich shares with us God's insight to her, namely that "all shall be well." Paul tells us that Jesus has robbed death of its power (2 Tim. 1:10).

Share, exchanging responses with one other person:
▲ Is it true to your experience that darkness is a natural part of the spiritual journey? Are you consoled by that? Why or why not?

The spiritual journey is one of growing in awareness of God's presence and action in our lives.

Anecdote: Jesuit Anthony DeMello told a story of a person who went to the town wise person and asked for a word of wisdom. "Could you tell me something that would guide me through my days?" he asked. The wise one said, "Awareness." The seeker paused and reflected. "Awareness?" he repeated. "This is too brief. Can you expand on it a bit?" The wise one responded, "Awareness, awareness, awareness." The seeker was confused. "But what does it mean?" he probed. The wise one answered: 'Awareness, awareness, awareness means—awareness."[5]

Expand: God initiated a love relationship with us, has promised to be with us always, and attempts to communicate with us through insights, people, events, feelings. God's self-revelation is ongoing, whether we're aware of it or not. Our openness to God's revelation provides us the richest blessings.

A. Our spiritual fathers and mothers all deliver variations of the same message: Be aware of God.
   1. Therese of Lisieux implores us to pay attention to our own experience of God's providential care.
   2. Meister Eckhart describes spirituality as waking up.
   3. Bernard Lanergan advises us to be attentive.
   4. Teresa of Avila calls us to be alert to God's action in life's unexpected events.
   5. John of the Cross wants us to be as aware of God as we are of the sun.
   6. Paul tells us to tune in to charity, which leads straight to God.

B. Everything has potential to manifest God to us if we're aware.

   Expand: God is constantly communicating with us. Because most of our life is ordinary, God speaks to us most often in ordinary ways through what is familiar to us. Parents have a wonderful opportunity to share with each other and with their children their own awareness of God's presence and action.

Share, exchanging responses with two or three others:

▲ Describe an event in your life that made you aware of God's presence and action.

1. God is in us and in other people.

   Expand: More than one family can share the story of a child who pointed in awe at the celebrant at Mass and exclaimed, "There's God!" Children have learned well that God is at church. The fundamental spiritual truth, however, that God is in their family members and those close to them is helpful to their growth in awareness of God.

2. God is in books.

   Expand: Many stories contain elements of the spiritual. Characters change in ways that reflect our own interior transformation. Conflicts are sometimes resolved by the use of discernment. Good usually overcomes evil. Themes are often scriptural. One or more of the characters often appear clothed in love, joy, peace, kindness, goodness, patience, faithfulness, gentleness, or self-control.

   Examples from children's literature:

   In *The Rag Coat* by Lauren Mills (Boston: Little, Brown and Company, 1991), Minna's classmates were transformed in ways similar to the Spirit transforming us.

   (Synopsis: Minna's classmates had teased her about her old coat, but were touched by hearing that their own parents had contributed some of the patches. With gentler hearts, they listened to Minna's stories, their stories, behind the patches. They acknowledged that they wouldn't blame Minna if she didn't want to be their friend. But the transformation was two-way. Minna and the children had a new respect for each other.)

   In *The Treasure* by Uri Shulevitz (Canada: Harper Collins, 1986), a poor man used discernment to solve his conflict.

   (Synopsis: In a recurring dream, a man traveled a long distance looking for treasure only to be advised to "look in the house of Isaac." Sure enough, the treasure had been close at hand all along, but had gone undiscovered until the man listened to his heart.)

   Good overcomes evil in *Tikvah Means Hope* by Patricia Polacco (New York: Bantam Doubleday Dell Books, 1994).

(Synopsis: After a devastating fire that caused widespread destruction and loss of life, the author witnessed the springing up of a sense of community in his neighborhood that "welded (our) spirits together" as neighbors helped one another recover from the loss.)

Lilly's Plastic Purse by Kevin Henkes (New York: Greenwillow Books, 1996) reflects the theme of forgiveness found in scripture: "Forgive as the Lord has forgiven you" (Col. 3:13).

(Synopsis: Mr. Slinger, Lilly's teacher, forgave her misbehavior in a note that said, "Today was a difficult day. Tomorrow will be better.")

In *I'm in Charge of Celebrations* by Byrd Baylor (New York: Aladdin Paperbacks, 1995) characters are clothed in the gifts of the Holy Spirit.

(Synopsis: Celebrations of the joy of creation fill this book. The main character honors creation with a special day of jubilation.)

Examples of adult literature:

In Jack Canfield and Mark Victor Hansen's *Chicken Soup for the Soul* (Deerfield Beach, Florida: Health Communications, Inc., 1993) numerous short stories tell of characters who manifest the gifts of the Holy Spirit. Testimonies of Spirit-filled people abound in this volume and its sequels.

Interior transformation takes place in Trudy, the main character in Ursula Hegi's *Stones from the River* (New York: Scribner Paperback Fiction, 1994), when she learns that "being different is a secret that all humans share." Set in a small town in Germany in the years prior to and during World War II, this story reveals the shadow side of most of the town's inhabitants as they interact with Trudy, the dwarf, an undesirable one. The change in Trudy occurs as she witnesses the history each of the others chooses to remember or forget.

Scriptural themes abound in *The Bean Trees* by Barbara Kingsolver. The protagonist, Taylor Greer, inherits a three-year-old American Indian girl in Oklahoma on her trip west. As Taylor's story as a mother unfolds, it reflects the words of Jesus: "I won't leave you like orphans. I will come back to you" (Jn. 14:18) and "Feed my lambs" (Jn. 21:15).

3. God is on television and in movies.

Expand: Some shows are overtly religious, but we can draw out the spiritual in those less obviously so. As families discuss programs together, parents can guide the process to highlight what spiritual elements there might be, as with books. This opens the eyes of family members to see the spiritual in the everyday. *(Television programming and movie releases change rapidly. The director might plan to find out what shows and films families are watching and prepare examples of how these programs or movies reflect spiritual messages, or ask the participants for examples.)*

4. God is in nature.

Anecdote: Many parents can remember fascinating ways their children made the link between God and nature. One parent tells of the time his son, upon hearing thunder, exclaimed, "I think God and the angels are bowling!" Another took her children into the mountains for a hike. In child-like wisdom, one of the children noticed, "You must have a big God inside you, Mommy. I'm little, so I have a little God inside me. Those flowers have a pretty God inside."

C. Spiritual discernment means recognizing the movement of God's Spirit in our lives.

Share, exchanging responses with the large group:
▲ Describe your awareness of God's presence and action in your life. Try to steer the conversation to focus on ordinary, rather than extraordinary, events.

Reflection for the week:
▲ How might I help my family see the spiritual in the ordinary?

Notes
1. Richard Hauser, S.J., *In His Spirit: A Guide to Today's Spirituality* (New York: Paulist Press, 1982), 26-36.
2. Ibid., 25.
3. Ibid., 36.
4. Moore, Thomas, *Care of the Soul* (New York: HarperCollins Publishers, 1992), 148.
5. DeMello, Anthony, *Awareness* (New York: Doubleday, 1990), 56.

Parent Session 5: Enjoying God

Note: The following parent talk is a basic outline with anecdotes, examples, points to expand, and questions to facilitate group interaction. It most likely contains more material than can be used. The director, therefore, should remain flexible and make changes according to the time limit of the adult retreat session. We recommend further that the director adapt the outline with personal examples, anecdotes relevant to the participants, and style of delivery that fits the director.

Focus

God wants us to enjoy God, a notion that is rooted in scripture. Developing a basic attitude of enjoyment about life in general will help us enjoy God. The language we choose to use and a positive mental outlook, for example, are ways we can develop an attitude of enjoyment. Prayer, too, can help us enjoy God as we examine the ways God has been present to us during the day.

The family is the primary place to learn to enjoy God. We enjoy God when we enjoy each other, the events we share, laughter and leisure. If we consider how Jesus led his life, we realize how many accounts revolved around his enjoying relationships: Jesus enjoying friends, Jesus enjoying the crowds, Jesus enjoying times of solitude with God. Laughter and leisure were at the heart of Jesus' ministry.

Laughter is spiritual and, as such, is medicine for wholeness. "Spiritual" means full of Spirit, that is love, peace, joy, patience, kindness, goodness, faithfulness, gentleness, and self-control. We've heard of people healing themselves by maintaining a bright, upbeat disposition throughout illness and adversity. We've seen people's intensity dissolve in laughter. Whenever people gather together socially, we hear laughter. This is Spirit. As we grow in the wholeness God wills for us, we increase our ability to infuse the Spirit's joyful gifts into all life.

Leisure has the potential to renew us and our families. In a culture that idealizes goal-setting and achievement, however, we can overlook the necessity of leisure. Lack of leisure at the expense of achievement takes its toll on our emotional and physical well-being. Many vacations, for instance, tightly packed with agendas, lack leisure, and people come back no healthier emotionally or physically than when they left. Building rituals of leisure into family life, on the other hand, can offer respite from the trap of overscheduling, and renew the spirit of joy and peace.

Outline

God wants us to enjoy God.

Anecdote: At a women's spirituality group the leader posed the question, "Do you enjoy God?" The long pause indicated most women were stumped by this. Love God? Yes. Honor God? Of course. But *enjoy* God? Hmmmm...

A. The notion of enjoying God is rooted in scripture.

1. "Be joyful and sing as you come in to worship the Lord!" (Ps. 100:2).

2. "But the angel said, 'Don't be afraid! I have good news for you, which will make everyone happy....a savior was born for you'" (Lk. 2:10-11).

3. Jesus tells his friends to live in his love and keep the commandments. "I have told you this to make you as completely happy as I am" (Jn. 15:7-11).

4. Ezra the priest-scribe called the people together to read them the law, then, because they were crying as they heard the words of the law, he said, "'Don't be sad. This is a special day for the Lord, and he will make you happy and strong.' ...When the people returned to their homes, they celebrated by eating and drinking and by sharing their food with those in need, because they had understood what had been read to them" (Neh. 8:8-12).

B. Developing a basic attitude of enjoyment will help us enjoy God.

1. Our language can influence how successfully we develop an attitude of enjoyment.

Anecdote: Karen is a vivacious young woman who has successfully developed an attitude of enjoyment. What's striking about Karen is that her vocabulary consistently expresses joy. "This is so much fun," or "I love doing this," are common expressions. What differentiates Karen's genuine Christian joy from a naive denial of reality is her stance that life will always be a mixed bag of joy and sorrow, and we can choose to highlight either one. Karen has chosen joy. Her expressions of joy are rooted in a disposition of gratitude. Contrast this to the extreme example of soap opera characters. Try turning off the sound, and watch the look of angst that pervades the screen. Enjoyment of God would be difficult to achieve for people who are so constantly miserable.

2. Our mental outlook influences our enjoyment level.

Expand: Mental health professionals advise us of healthy ways to rise above negative experiences and consequent negative responses. One way to increase our enjoyment level in the face of adversity is to reach out to people. Another is to always have something to look forward to. A man who had suffered the loss of his wife, for example, found consolation in spending holidays serving the poor in a soup kitchen. A church mothers' group sponsors frequent "Moms' Nights Out" to provide at least monthly occasions to look forward to for those who occasionally feel overwhelmed by family responsibilities.

3. Our prayer can help us enjoy God.

Expand: St. Ignatius of Loyola, the founder of the Jesuits, suggested the daily prayer of Examen of Consciousness as the most important way to remain centered in God. It is also a marvelous way to enjoy God. The examen is a review of how God has been present in events, people, and feelings throughout the day, week, or year. In this prayer, we speak to God following the "dynamic of personal love: what we always want to say to a person whom we truly love in the order in which we want to say it....Thank you....Help me....I love you....I'm sorry....Be with me."[1]

Another suggestion spiritual directors sometimes make is to prayerfully review each day by asking God these questions: Where did I see your face today? How did you touch my heart today? A third prayer that many find helpful is to create a mantra (eg., "Fill me with your joy" or "I enjoy you, loving God"), saying it often at first, then less and less as its reality becomes a part of us.

Pray: Lead participants in a time of reflection, following one of the suggestions above. Allow approximately two minutes. Invite retreatants to share their experience afterwards with one other person.

C. The family is the prime place to learn to enjoy God.
   1. We enjoy God when we enjoy each other.

Expand: Our relationships with the people we are closest to mirror our relationship with God. Richard Hauser, S.J., author of *In His Spirit,* points out that "we cannot be united with the God of love in prayer without simultaneously becoming more loving in action. During all his writing Paul shows that this love, 'the love of God... poured out into our hearts by the Holy Spirit which has been given us' (Romans 5:5) directs us equally to God and to one another. The love for each will be equal since it flows from the same source in us, the Holy Spirit. Jesus himself emphasized the unity of the two loves in our lives by insisting that the two great commandments of love of God and love of neighbor were equal."[2]

Anecdote: Brett is a young adult who loves his family but dreads returning for vacations. His visits are burdened with a sense of obligation. When the family gets together they speak negatively, criticize, and argue with each other, as they have since he was a child—that is, unless an outsider is present. So Brett has learned to bring a friend each time in an effort to enjoy his visits more. Not so coincidentally, Brett tells his spiritual director of his difficulty relating to God. He aches for a loving, joyful relationship, but perceives God as unreliable and seemingly capricious in doling out love. Brett has trouble enjoying God just as he does relating to his family. He knows intellectually that both love him, but he's tentative about entering into that love.

Share, exchanging responses with the large group:
▲ How do we as parents create the kind of home adult children want to return to?

2. We enjoy God through the events we enjoy.

Expand: Many parents decry the commercial nature of holidays, and with good reason. It's far too easy to overlook the spiritual in these special days. However, it's possible to combine the spiritual and temporal, creating enjoyable events where families learn to enjoy God, too. Being Christian should not be dry, somber, and academic. To turn Christmas or birthdays into theological castor oil as an antidote to commercialism does not adequately address the message the scriptures repeat, to live a joyful life. Families might instead celebrate a child's birthday festively and joyously, all the while repeating (approximately) the words God spoke through the prophet Isaiah: "You are precious to us and we love you. We're so glad you were born. We're so glad you are ours" (Isa. 43:1-4).

At Christmas, the waiting can be an exciting time for families. Parties are not only a prelude to the birth of Christ, but are also a sign of the love and intimacy among people that Jesus represents. Santa Claus shares many qualities with God, and the similarity need only be mentioned for children to recognize it.

Share, exchanging responses with the large group:
▲ How have you successfully made holidays joyful, spiritual events?

3. We enjoy God in laughter and leisure.

Expand: Consider how Jesus led his life. The accounts we read revolve around relationships: Jesus enjoying friends, Jesus enjoying the crowds,

Jesus enjoying times of solitude with God. Laughter and leisure in Jesus' life were at the heart of his ministry of presence. In his life, "being" was more important than "doing."

Examples: On more than one occasion, Jesus invited his apostles to go away with him and rest (Mk. 6:31-33). Jesus spent time with his friends Martha and Mary (Lk. 10:38-42). One of Jesus' last times with his apostles was at a meal where he washed their feet (Jn. 13).

Laughter is spiritual

Expand: "Spiritual" means full of Spirit: love, peace, joy, patience, kindness, goodness, faithfulness, gentleness, and self-control.

A. Laughter helps us heal.

Expand: We've heard of people healing themselves by maintaining a bright, upbeat disposition throughout illness and adversity. We've seen intensity dissolve in laughter. Whenever people gather together socially, we hear laughter. In wholeness, which God wills for us, we embrace suffering in healthy ways, one of which is laughter, when appropriate.

B. Laughter removes barriers to the Spirit's gifts of love, peace, and joy.

Expand: Life can contain both joy and suffering. Suffering requires compassion, but sometimes a light heart can heal just as well.

Anecdote: A woman was complaining to a friend about a particular habit of her husband's that annoyed her enormously. Caterin was so irritated, she felt like this obstacle could endanger her marriage. All of a sudden her friend laughed. Caterin was confused. "That sounds so much like me," chuckled her friend. To her surprise Caterin felt relieved. Her friend's light-hearted perception was just what she needed to restore peace, love, and joy.

C. Laughter helps us enjoy God.

Expand: When we are full of joy, we are full of God, and we radiate God to other people. The beauty and goodness of laughter, the release of tension and anxiety that results, the renewal and healing it effects are reminders of God's own joy.

Anecdote: When asked to describe her family for a class at school, one young girl said, "We laugh a lot." The teacher asked her to say more. "It usually happens while we're still hanging around the kitchen after dinner. Once we get started, everything seems funny. It's kind of silly, but it feels good." Dolores

Curran, in her book *Traits of the Healthy Family,* cites laughter, including "inside jokes," as a quality healthy families share.[3] Laughter can dissipate tensions, stress, and even the doldrums, and bring alive in the family the joy that God wills for us.

Share, exchanging responses with two or three others:

▲ What does laughter do for you that's "of God"?

The spirituality of leisure can be dangerously overlooked in the mentality of goal-setting and achievement.

A. A crucial question to ask ourselves is, "At what price do I want achievement?"

1. Ecclesiates (2:1-12), who makes pointed statements about the vanity of all things throughout his treatise, examines this same question.

   Expand: Read parts or all of Eccl. 2:1-12. After Ecclesiastes announces that he "undertook great works" (v. 4), he concludes, "But when I turned to all the works that my hands had wrought, and to the toil at which I had taken such pains, behold! all was vanity and a chase after wind, with nothing gained under the sun" (v. 11).

2. Lack of leisure takes its toll on our emotional and physical well-being.

   Anecdote: Two friends on vacation were leisurely viewing a spectacular waterfall. They were so taken with the view that they stayed for three hours. During that time, they witnessed countless people walk up, stand for several minutes, then announce, "Well, let's get going. We have more to see." Many vacations lack leisure, and people come back no healthier emotionally or physically than when they left.

   Anecdote: Twelve-year-old Andrew and his family were returning from spring break at Disneyland. School would resume the next day. While Andrew's mother was reminiscing about the attractions, Andrew interrupted: "I don't want to ruin my vacation like this ever again. I had a good time and everything, but my vacation's ruined. I had no time to do nothing."

3. Leisure has the potential to renew us and our families.

   Expand: What affects one member of the family affects all. If one member is stressed because of too little leisure, the dynamics of the family are affected.

   Anecdote: One family described how they found great healing during the duration of a family vacation because the respite gave the father much needed and long-overdue leisure. Once refreshed and renewed, he related differently to family members, and they to each other. Sadly, though, old habits resumed after the vacation. The father continued to deny himself leisure in an effort to achieve his goals, and lost an opportunity to bring balance to the family.

B. Modern families complain of too little time together.

Expand: Dolores Curran addresses this issue in her books *Traits of the Healthy Family*[4] and *Stress and the Healthy Family.*[5] Not only do families have adults working long hours in attempts to achieve goals, but children, too, have packed schedules. Most athletic teams, for example, require at least one practice and one game per week. If several children are on this schedule, the family can be torn apart rather than united.

C. Building rituals into family life can offer respite from the trap of overscheduling.

Expand: Inviting each child to take a turn enjoying special time with a parent, even something as simple as running an errand together or pounding nails with one another (something fun, not drudgery!), helps create leisurely times together. Some families set aside Sunday morning for family time, which includes a fun or fancy breakfast after Mass. Invite participants to add ideas by responding to this question:

▲ What's your favorite family ritual?

Reflection for the week:

▲ Do we have a healthy balance of laughter and leisure in our family?

▲ What modifications could we make to create this balance?

Notes

1. Marian Cowan and John Futrell, *The Spiritual Exercises of St. Ignatius of Loyola: A Handbook for Directors* (New York: Le Jacq Publishing, 1982), 34-35, quoted in Jacqueline Syrup Bergan and S. Marie Schwan, *Love: A Guide for Prayer* (Winona, Minn.: St. Mary's Press, 1985), 7.
2. Richard Hauser S.J., *In His Spirit: A Guide to Today's Spirituality* (New York: Paulist Press, 1982), 104.
3. Dolores Curran, *Traits of the Healthy Family* (New York: Ballantine, 1983).
4. *Ibid.*
5. Dolores Curran, *Stress and the Healthy Family* (New York: HarperCollins, 1987).

Appendix

Letters to Parents

1-Eucharist Retreat

(1 Corinthians 12:4-31)

Dear Family,

I made a retreat today and I came away with four important thoughts to remember:

▲ When we receive the Eucharist, we receive Jesus under the appearance of bread and wine. We become united with Jesus, and he with us.

▲ Because we are united with Jesus, we see Jesus in each other.

▲ Each of us is a message of love from God to everyone else.

▲ When we are with each other in love we are the Body of Christ.

The scripture the retreat was based on was 1 Corinthians 12:4-31. Can we look it up together right now?

But the retreat isn't over yet. I'd like to share my experience with you before I feel my retreat is complete.

One of the activities was reading a story and trying to recognize what character in the story was most like Jesus. The story we read, *Old Turtle* by Douglas Wood, was about how the creatures of the earth argued among themselves about who or what God was. Some thought God was gentle; others, powerful. Some believed God was above all things; others, within all things. Old Turtle said that soon there would be a wonderful new family of beings in the world and that they would be a message of love from God to the earth and a prayer from the earth back to God.

Ask me to tell you about the character I thought was most like Jesus, and why. Can you help me think of ways I can be more like this character, and thus more like Jesus, this week?

We learned that God dwells within us. Because of that, we can pray by going deep inside ourselves to a quiet place where Jesus is. Some people call this the Heart Room. We closed our eyes, sat quietly, and imagined ourselves going to this place to meet Jesus. I spent time looking at him, then I talked to him. Ask me what he looked like and what I said to him. Ask me if he said anything to me. Encourage me to pray in my heart room whenever I feel happy or scared, sad or alone. I would like it if we could pray this way together sometimes. Could we take a few minutes and try it now? I'll show you how.

Our third activity was to make a souvenir of the retreat to bring home. I'll show you my Body of Christ Grocery Bag Vest. Part of it isn't finished yet, and I want to invite you to finish it with me by adding the words "We see God in each other." This souvenir reminds me of one message of the retreat: When we are with each other in love we are the Body of Christ.

2-Reconciliation Retreat

(Matthew 18:10-14; Luke 23:34)

Dear Family,

On my retreat today I came away with four important thoughts to remember:

▲ Because God made us, we are good. However, we may do bad things.

▲ In the sacrament of Reconciliation, we are reunited with God and each other.

▲ When God forgives us, God brings us back into a loving relationship where we feel more peaceful, better about ourselves, and want to live a more loving life again.

▲ Because God forgives us endlessly in our sinfulness, we learn to forgive others in the same way.

The scriptures the retreat was based on were Matthew 18:10-14 and Luke 23:34. Can we look these up together right now?

But the retreat isn't over yet. I'd like to share my experience with you before I feel my retreat is complete. One of the activities was reading a story and trying to recognize what character in the story was most like Jesus. The story we read, *Lilly's Purple Plastic Purse* by Kevin Henkes, about a girl who brings her purse to school, and has it taken away because she it disrupts the class. Wanting to get back at her teacher, Lilly draws an unflattering picture of him. But at the end of the day, the teacher returns the purse—with a friendly note and tasty snacks inside. Through this experience, Lilly learns about reconciliation. In return, she writes the teacher a note and makes him some treats. Ask me to tell you about the character I thought was most like Jesus, and why. Can you help me think of ways I can be more like this character, and thus more like Jesus, this week?

We learned that God dwells within us. Because of that, we can pray by going deep inside ourselves to a quiet place where Jesus is. Some people call this the Heart Room. We closed our eyes, sat quietly, and imagined ourselves going to this place to meet Jesus. I spent time looking at him, then I talked to him. Ask me what he looked like and what I said to him. Ask me if he said anything to me. Encourage me to pray in my heart room whenever I feel happy or scared, sad or alone. I would like it if we could pray this way together sometimes. Could we take a few minutes and try it now? I'll show you how.

Our third activity was to make a souvenir of the retreat to bring home. I'll show you my Peace Partner Reconciliation board game. Part of it isn't finished yet, and I want to invite you to finish decorating the outside of the game with me. Let's play it together. This souvenir reminds me of the message of the retreat: Because God forgives us, we forgive others.

3-Good Friends Retreat

(Matthew 4:18-22)

Dear Family,

I made a retreat today and I came away with three important thoughts to remember:

▲ Through everything that happens in our life, good or bad, Jesus is there.

▲ We are a presence of God's love to the people in our lives.

▲ By being good friends with others, we become better friends with Jesus.

The scripture the retreat was based on was Matthew 4:18-22. Can we look it up together right now?

But the retreat isn't over yet. I'd like to share my experience with you before I feel my retreat is complete.

One of the activities was reading a story and trying to recognize what character in the story was most like Jesus. The story we read, *In God's Name* by Sandy Eisenberg Sasso, was about the many ways people understand God. In the story, the people knelt by a lake that was "God's mirror." I learned from this that we mirror God's love to the people in our lives.

Ask me to tell you about how the story referred to the spirit of God alive in people. Can you help me this week to show my family and friends the spirit of God in me?

We learned that God dwells within us. Because of that, we can pray by going deep inside ourselves to a quiet place where Jesus is. Some people call this the Heart Room. We closed our eyes, sat quietly, and imagined ourselves going to this place to meet Jesus. I spent time looking at him, then I talked to him. Ask me what he looked like and what I said to him. Ask me if he said anything to me. Encourage me to pray in my heart room whenever I feel happy or scared, sad or alone. I would like it if we could pray this way together sometimes. Could we take a few minutes and try it now? I'll show you how.

Our third activity was to make a souvenir of the retreat to bring home. I'll show you my Jesus Zipper-Bag Book. It holds mementos of my retreat, which I'd like to show you. This souvenir reminds me of one message of the retreat: Through everything that happens in our lives, good or bad, Jesus is there.

188

4-Good News Retreat

(Luke 10:21; Mattthew 19:13; Matthew 18:1-5; 1 John 4:10, 19)

Dear Family,

I made a retreat today and I came away with four important thoughts to remember:

- ▲ We use the expression "Good News" when we talk about all that God's love means to us.
- ▲ An important aspect of God's love is that God loved us first (1 Jn. 4:10, 19).
- ▲ One way God shows love to us is through people we meet.
- ▲ It takes practice recognizing when and how God is making God's love known to us.

The scriptures the retreat was based on were Lk. 10:21, Mt. 19:13, Mt. 18:1-5, and 1 Jn. 4:10, 19. Can we look these up together right now?

But the retreat isn't over yet. I'd like to share my experience with you before I feel my retreat is complete.

One of the activities was reading a story and trying to recognize what character in the story was most like Jesus. The story we read, *Ming Lo Moves the Mountain* by Arnold Lobel, was about a man and woman who wanted to move the mountain that brought rain on their house. They sought the help of a wise man, who taught them the dance of the moving mountain. But what he really showed them was that to move the mountain, they had to move themselves.

Ask me to tell you about the character I thought was most like Jesus, and why. Can you help me think of ways I can be more like this character, and thus more like Jesus, this week?

We learned that God dwells within us. Because of that, we can pray by going deep inside ourselves to a quiet place where Jesus is. Some people call this the Heart Room. We closed our eyes, sat quietly, and imagined ourselves going to this place to meet Jesus. I spent time looking at him, then I talked to him. Ask me what he looked like and what I said to him. Ask me if he said anything to me. Encourage me to pray in my heart room whenever I feel happy or scared, sad or alone. I would like it if we could pray this way together sometimes. Could we take a few minutes and try it now? I'll show you how.

Our third activity was to make a souvenir of the retreat to bring home. I'll show you my bubbles. If we want to make more, I can show you how. This souvenir reminds me of the message of the retreat: the good news that God loves me bubbles up inside me.

5-The Great Commandment Retreat

(John 15:15-16; 1 John 4:19; Mattthew 22:37-39)

Dear Family,

On my retreat today, I came away with four important thoughts to remember:

▲ Jesus told us to love God, each other, and ourselves.

▲ Our relationship with ourselves and our relationship with others mirror our relationship with God.

▲ Loving ourselves might seem like bragging, but it's not. We can't love each other if we don't love ourselves.

▲ The people we like to be around—the ones who are the most like Jesus—are people who love themselves.

The scriptures the retreat was based on were Jn. 15:15-16, 1 Jn. 4:19, and Mt. 22:37-39. Can we look these up together right now? But the retreat isn't over yet. I'd like to share my experience with you before I feel my retreat is complete.

One of the activities was reading a story and trying to recognize what character in the story was most like Jesus. The story we read, *Love You Forever* by Robert Munsch, was about a parent's enduring love. When the boy in the story passed from childhood into adulthood, he brought to the next generation the love his mother had shown him. Ask me to tell you about the character I thought was most like Jesus, and why. Can you help me think of ways I can be more like this character, and thus more like Jesus, this week?

We learned that God dwells within us. Because of that, we can pray by going deep inside ourselves to a quiet place where Jesus is. Some people call this the Heart Room. We closed our eyes, sat quietly, and imagined ourselves going to this place to meet Jesus. I spent time looking at him, then I talked to him. Ask me what he looked like and what I said to him. Ask me if he said anything to me. Encourage me to pray in my heart room whenever I feel happy or scared, sad or alone. I would like it if we could pray this way together sometimes. Could we take a few minutes and try it now? I'll show you how.

Our third activity was to make a souvenir of the retreat to bring home: my scrapbook. Part of it isn't finished yet, and I want to invite you to finish it with me by taping or gluing something into it or by drawing something on the back cover to show your support. Ask me what words encourage me. Write them somewhere in my scrapbook. Tell me some words that encourage you. I'll write those in my scrapbook. Let's say these words to each other this week. This souvenir reminds me of the message of the retreat: I want to love God, myself, and others.

6-Come As You Are Retreat

(Luke 2:41-52; Psalm 142:2-3; Psalm 44:3-7)

Dear Family,

On my retreat today, I came away with three important thoughts to remember:

▲ There's nothing we can do or say that will make Jesus go away.

▲ Jesus loves us at least as much as the person who loves us the most.

▲ We can share all our feelings with God—angry, glad, sad, or scared—just as Job and the psalmists did.

The scriptures the retreat was based on were Lk. 2:41-52, Ps. 142:2-3, and Ps. 44:3-7. Can we look these up together right now? But the retreat isn't over yet. I'd like to share my experience with you before I feel my retreat is complete.

One of the activities was reading a story and trying to recognize what character in the story was most like Jesus. The story we read, *The Velveteen Rabbit* by Margery Williams, was about a stuffed rabbit who belonged to a family for generations and was loved until it looked shabby. Its greatest desire was to become real. Once you are real, he learned, you can't be ugly except to people who don't understand.

Ask me to tell you about the character I thought was most like Jesus, and why. Can you help me think of ways I can be more like this character, and thus more like Jesus, this week?

We learned that God dwells within us. Because of that, we can pray by going deep inside ourselves to a quiet place where Jesus is. Some people call this the Heart Room. We closed our eyes, sat quietly, and imagined ourselves going to this place to meet Jesus. I spent time looking at him, then I talked to him. Ask me what he looked like and what I said to him. Ask me if he said anything to me. Encourage me to pray in my heart room whenever I feel happy or scared, sad or alone. I would like it if we could pray this way together sometimes. Could we take a few minutes and try it now? I'll show you how.

Our third activity was to make a souvenir of the retreat to bring home. I'll show you my filmstrip picture frame. Part of it isn't finished yet, and I want to invite you to finish it with me. This souvenir reminds me of the message of the retreat: We can share all of our feelings with God. On one section I've written *The retreat continues*. Ask me about my easiest feelings to share with God. Tell me yours. Let's talk about feelings that might be difficult for both of us to share with God. Together let's write or draw something in the final section of the filmstrip. Then we can hang it in a special place in my room or wherever we think it would go best.

7-Respect Retreat

(Matthew 14:28-31; John 6:1-13)

Dear Family,

I made a retreat today and I came away with three important thoughts to remember:

▲ Wherever there is love, Jesus is there.

▲ Love means respecting, accepting, and honoring people just as they are.

▲ Yet love does not require us to be treated badly by others.

The scriptures the retreat was based on were Mt. 14:28-31 and Jn. 6:1-13. Can we look these up together right now?

But the retreat isn't over yet. I'd like to share my experience with you before I feel my retreat is complete.

One of the activities was reading a story and trying to recognize what character in the story was most like Jesus. The story we read, *People* by Peter Spier, was about the uniqueness of people all over the world, their language, appearance, clothing, food and customs. It advocated acceptance, respect, and honor for all of humankind. We talked about how Jesus wasn't afraid to be with people of his time who were different, like tax collectors, lepers, and people with disabilities. Can you help me think of ways I can be more like Jesus in accepting people who are different from me this week?

We learned that God dwells within us. Because of that, we can pray by going deep inside ourselves to a quiet place where Jesus is. Some people call this the Heart Room. We closed our eyes, sat quietly, and imagined ourselves going to this place to meet Jesus. I spent time looking at him, then I talked to him. Ask me what he looked like and what I said to him. Ask me if he said anything to me. Encourage me to pray in my heart room whenever I feel happy or scared, sad or alone. I would like it if we could pray this way together sometimes. Could we take a few minutes and try it now? I'll show you how.

Our third activity was to make a souvenir of the retreat to bring home. I'll show you my sit upon/prayer pillow. Part of it isn't finished yet, and I want to invite you to finish it with me by helping me make a pillowcase or cover for it. We can sew, staple, or tape together pieces of an old shower curtain, vinyl tablecloth, or plastic grocery sack. Two bandanas would work, too, or we could come up with a different idea. I can use it for picnics or camping, or for prayer time with Jesus. This souvenir reminds me of the message of the retreat: Love means accepting, honoring, and respecting people as they are.

8-Shining Light Retreat

(Luke 11:33-36)

Dear Family,

I made a retreat today and I came away with three important thoughts to remember:

- ▲ God dwells within us.
- ▲ Because of this, people can see Jesus if we allow Jesus to shine forth
- ▲ We're good because of our friendship with Jesus. Being good means people feel good when they're with us because we're so much like Jesus.

The scripture the retreat was based on was Lk. 11:33-36. Can we look it up together right now?

But the retreat isn't over yet. I'd like to share my experience with you before I feel my retreat is complete.

One of the activities was reading a story and trying to recognize what character in the story was most like Jesus. The story we read, *The Boy Who Held Back the Sea* by Thomas Locker, was about a boy named Jan who was often mischievous, but who changed when he saw his town was in danger of a flood. Wanting to do the right thing, he saved everybody in his town by holding his hand in the dike.

Ask me to tell you about the character I thought was most like Jesus, and why. Can you help me think of ways I can be more like this character, and thus more like Jesus, this week?

We learned that God dwells within us. Because of that, we can pray by going deep inside ourselves to a quiet place where Jesus is. Some people call this the Heart Room. We closed our eyes, sat quietly, and imagined ourselves going to this place to meet Jesus. I spent time looking at him, then I talked to him. Ask me what he looked like and what I said to him. Ask me if he said anything to me. Encourage me to pray in my heart room whenever I feel happy or scared, sad or alone. I would like it if we could pray this way together sometimes. Could we take a few minutes and try it now? I'll show you how.

Our third activity was to make a souvenir of the retreat to bring home. I'll show you my Cardboard Tube Kazoo. Part of it isn't finished yet, and I want to invite you to finish it with me. This souvenir reminds me of the message of the retreat because music lights me up inside. When I shine, the love of Jesus shines through me.

9-Presence Retreat

(Luke 1:26; Luke 2:8-20)

Dear Family,

I made a retreat today and I came away with four important thoughts to remember:

- ▲ The word Incarnation means that God's son became human like us.
- ▲ As a person living among us, Jesus was a messenger of God's love, as we are.
- ▲ Jesus is still present to us, in the ordinary things of life.
- ▲ Stillness helps us be close to Jesus because it allows us time to notice Jesus and to listen to what Jesus might want to say to us.

The scriptures the retreat was based on were Lk. 1:26 and Lk. 2:8-20. Can we look these up together right now?

But the retreat isn't over yet. I'd like to share my experience with you before I feel my retreat is complete.

One of the activities was reading a story and trying to recognize what character in the story was most like Jesus. The story we read, *Sylvester and the Magic Pebble* by William Steig, was about a donkey who asked his magic pebble to turn him into a rock, but then couldn't hold the pebble to wish himself back to normal again. Ask me how Sylvester was eventually reunited with his parents and restored to his authentic self. Ask me also to tell you about the character I thought was most like Jesus, and why. Can you help me think of ways I can be more like this character, and thus more like Jesus, this week?

We learned that God dwells within us. Because of that, we can pray by going deep inside ourselves to a quiet place where Jesus is. Some people call this the Heart Room. We closed our eyes, sat quietly, and imagined ourselves going to this place to meet Jesus. I spent time looking at him, then I talked to him. Ask me what he looked like and what I said to him. Ask me if he said anything to me. Encourage me to pray in my heart room whenever I feel happy or scared, sad or alone. I would like it if we could pray this way together sometimes. Could we take a few minutes and try it now? I'll show you how.

Our third activity was to make a souvenir of the retreat to bring home. I'll show you my Draw-a-Prayer with foil and string frame. Part of it isn't finished yet, and I want to invite you to finish it with me. This souvenir reminds me of the message of the retreat: during this busy season of the year, I don't want to forget Jesus. Stillness allows us time to listen to Jesus.

Eucharist Retreat
Souvenir

Suggestions of people in the Body of Christ who can be included on the vest souvenir.

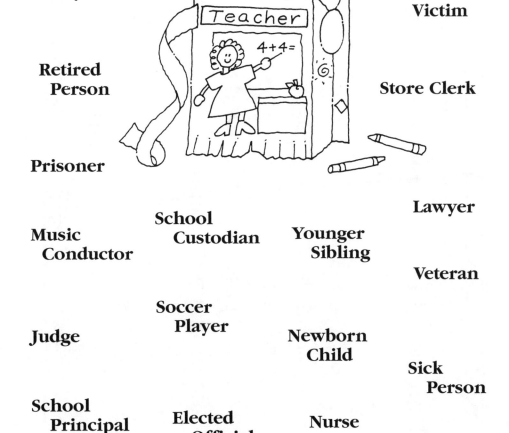

Babysitter

Accident Victim

Retired Person

Store Clerk

Prisoner

Lawyer

Music Conductor

School Custodian

Younger Sibling

Veteran

Judge

Soccer Player

Newborn Child

Sick Person

School Principal

Elected Official

Nurse

College Student

Policewoman

Homeless Person

Reconciliation Retreat
Gathering Presentation

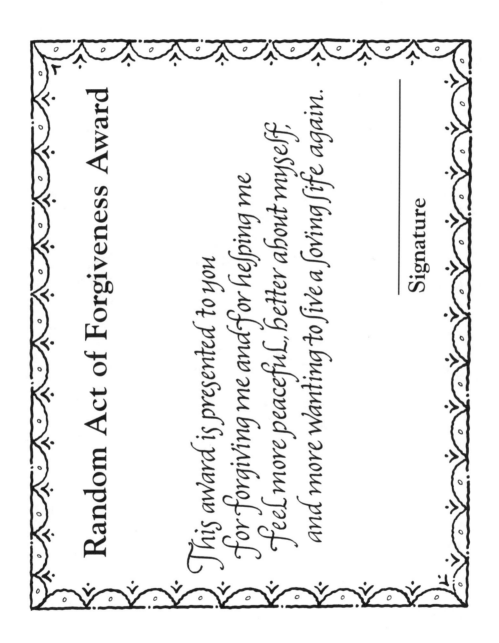

Random Act of Forgiveness Award

This award is presented to you
for forgiving me and for helping me
feel more peaceful, better about myself,
and more wanting to live a loving life again.

_____

Signature

Reconciliation Retreat

Souvenir

(Enlarge on copy machine to 8 1/2" x 11".)

Reconciliation Retreat

Souvenir

(Enlarge on copy machine to 8 1/2" x 11".)

Reconciliation Retreat

Souvenir

(Enlarge on copy machine to 8 1/2" x 11".)

Good Friends Retreat

Gathering Presentation

JESUS' LIFE-GIVING FRIENDSHIP IS FRIEND HELPS BEST FRIEND

David and Marissa were best friends. Jesus is our best friend. One day they were hiking when suddenly David lost his footing and tumbled down the cliff. Sometimes, when we feel scared, darkness grabs us like a kidnapper with a gunny sack. His fear gripped at him like a surgeon holding a throbbing appendix. But in everything that happens in our life, good and bad, our special friend Jesus is there. Marissa reached out and saved him. His friendship is life-giving. David realized he had the best friend a person could ever want.

Possible Solutions

Adventure Magazine

FRIEND HELPS BEST FRIEND

David and Marissa were best friends. One day they were hiking when suddenly David lost his footing and tumbled down the cliff. His fear gripped at him like a surgeon holding a throbbing appendix. Marissa reached out and saved him. David realized he had the best friend a person could ever want.

Religious Magazine

JESUS' FRIENDSHIP IS LIFE-GIVING

Jesus is our best friend. Sometimes, when we feel scared, darkness grabs us like a kidnapper with a gunny sack. But in everything that happens in our life, good and bad, our special friend Jesus is there. His friendship is life-giving.

For overhead or magnetic strips:

(Adventure Magazine)

FRIEND HELPS BEST FRIEND

David and Marissa were best friends.

One day they were hiking when suddenly David lost his footing and tumbled down the cliff.

His fear gripped at him like a surgeon holding a throbbing appendix.

Marissa reached out and saved him.

David realized he had the best friend a person could ever want.

(Religious Magazine)

JESUS' FRIENDSHIP IS LIFE-GIVING

Jesus is our best friend.

Sometimes, when we feel scared, darkness grabs us like a kidnapper with a gunny sack.

But in everything that happens in our life, good and bad, our special friend Jesus is there.

His friendship is life-giving.

Good Friends Retreat

Souvenir

The title of the book I heard
was

_____

The author was

_____

This picture will help me
recall the story.

(Enlarge each page to the size of zipper bag.)

Good Friends Retreat

Souvenir

> This sketch reminds me
> that I can talk to Jesus in
> my heart anytime.

(Enlarge each page to the size of zipper bag.)

Good Friends Retreat

Story as Prayer

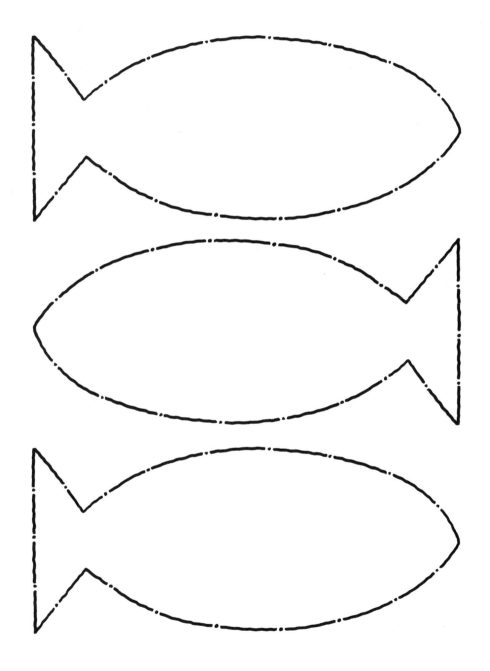

(Enlarge on copy machine to 8 1/2" x 11".)

Good News Retreat
Souvenir

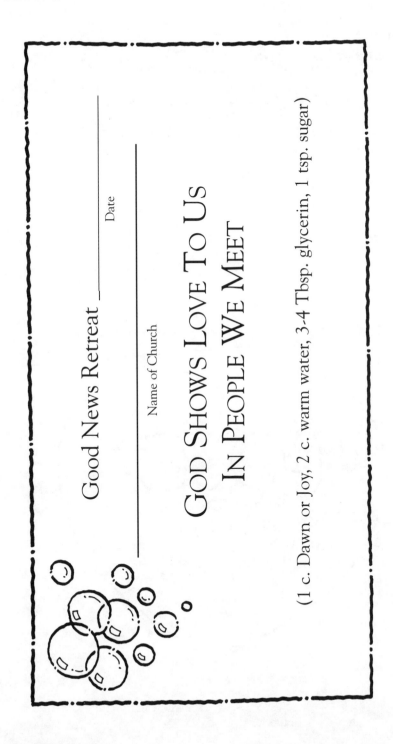

Good News Retreat

Date

Name of Church

GOD SHOWS LOVE TO US
IN PEOPLE WE MEET

(1 c. Dawn or Joy, 2 c. warm water, 3-4 Tbsp. glycerin, 1 tsp. sugar)

(Enlarge to 4 1/2" x 8 1/2".)

Great Commandment Retreat
Nametag

Heart Room
Prayer Activity

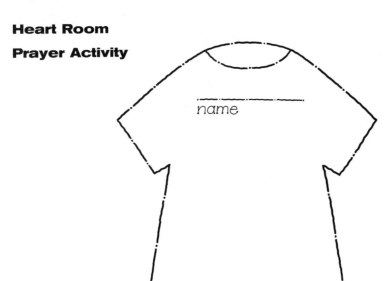

Souvenir

(Enlarge each picture to 8 1/2" x 11".)

Great Commandment Retreat
Souvenir

Love Myself

(Enlarge each picture to 8 1/2" x 11".)

Great Commandment Retreat
Souvenir

Love
People

(Enlarge to 8 1/2" x 11".)

Great Commandment Retreat

Souvenir

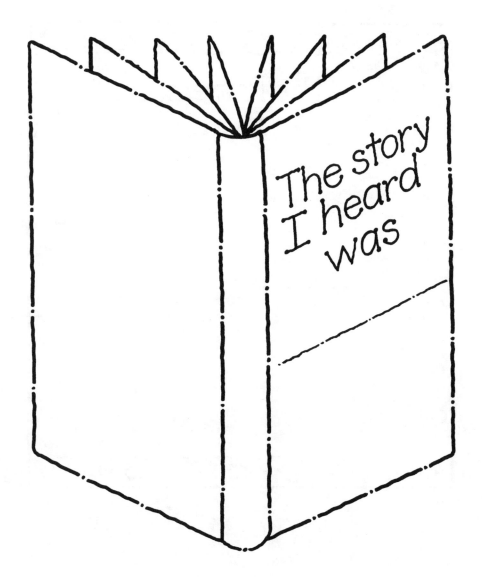

The story I heard was

(Enlarge to 8 1/2" x 11".)

Great Commandment Retreat

Souvenir

The Retreat Continues!

(Enlarge to 8 1/2" x 11".)

Respect Retreat

Heart Room Prayer — Icthys

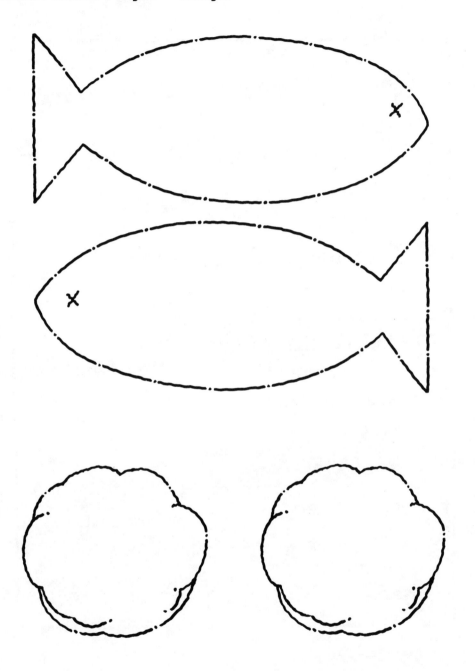

(Enlarge to 8 1/2" x 11".)

Respect Retreat

Church Name   Date

_____   _____

Jesus told us to love God, each other
and ourselves. Our relationship with
ourselves and our relationship with
others mirror our relationship with
God. Loving ourselves might seem
like bragging, but it's not. We can't
love each other if we don't love
ourselves.

(Enlarge to size of zipper bag.)

Parent Sessions

Heart Room Prayer

"Close your eyes and place your feet comfortably on the floor, hands relaxed in your lap. *(pause)* Pay attention to your breathing. *(pause)* As you breathe in, breathe in the love of God. As you breathe out, breathe out anything that might prevent you from focusing on God's love. *(pause)* Breathe in God's love; breathe out any barriers to God's love. *(pause)* As you breathe in, breathe in God's peace. And as you breathe out, breathe out any anxiety or worry. *(pause)* Breathe in God's peace; breathe out anxiety."

Wait 30 seconds, then continue:

"Visualize yourself moving down, now, into that most intimate, private place, which is your own heart. *(pause)* You hear a knock on the door of your heart, a door that can only be opened from the inside. You know who is knocking. It's Jesus. Go to the door and welcome Jesus in your own way."

Wait 30 seconds.

"Invite Jesus into your heart room if you can. If you can't, tell him so, openly and honestly.

"Sit with Jesus now, or speak to him from a distance if you're more comfortable. Tell him what's in your heart."

Wait 1-2 minutes.

"Now close this time with Jesus. Ask him to stay with you, to dwell there in your heart room where you can always meet him."

Pause 30 seconds.

Ask each person to share with one other person something that happened in their prayer. For many, this may be the first time they've shared a faith experience. This will help them share more easily with their children later.

Adult-Child Sharing Form

To set the tone for quality sharing time between adults and children, duplicate this explanation and questions.

It's time now to join your child for individual sharing of your experiences today. The children have had four experiences of prayer.

▲ They've made a craft, a _____.

▲ While the children were constructing it, they talked about_____.

▲ They heard the story_____by_____. It's about_____. Afterwards, they talked about the spiritual meaning of the story:_____.

▲ They visited Jesus in their heart room, as you did. The adult leader led the children in their imaginations to_____ where the_____. Afterwards, they said whatever they wanted to their best friend Jesus, in their heart rooms.

▲ They broke bread together, just as Jesus often did with his friends. Their snack was _____.

Your children may need questions to get them started sharing. Here are some suggestions.

▲ Tell me about the story you heard.
▲ What do you like about the craft you made?
▲ What was it like when you met Jesus in your heart room?
▲ What did Jesus look like?
▲ How did it feel to be with Jesus?
▲ When I met Jesus in my heart room, he said... I did...
▲ What did Jesus say to you? What did you do?